GORING AND FERRING

PAST AND PRESENT

Written and Compiled by
John Vaughan

GORING HALL DRIVE, FERRING—BY—SEA.

R.A.P. Co. Ltd.,
London.

Plate 1. There are many links between Goring and Ferring. Although they are geographically joined the primary topographical features shared are the South Downs and Highdown Hill, the beach and the coastline and the delightful Goring Hall Drive. This 1933 postcard shows the west to east view between the mature Ilex trees, often referred to as Mediterranean or Evergreen Oaks. This is one of the few postcards to show both Goring and Ferring in the caption.

Dedication
To my Mother, Ethel Vaughan
Humble and modest,
Loving and honest,
Simply the best!
Thank you for everything

Plate 2. One of the great joys of the area is Highdown Hill where ramblers and dog walkers can enjoy views from the Isle of Wight to Beachy Head. In Spring the magnificent drive is lined by a brilliant display of daffodils. At the top of the drive is Highdown Towers which from 1909 until 1972 was the Stern family home. Sir Frederick Stern died in 1967 and Lady Sybil Stern in 1972. The 1820 built house was bequeathed to the local authority and later leased to the Institute of Choreology but with finance the all important driver the house became a night club which subsequently attracted adverse publicity. The fine chalk garden, created by Sir Frederick Stern, which was so admired by the Prince of Wales during his 1933 visit, is open to the public and beautifully maintained by Worthing Borough Council.

PHOTOGRAPHS All modern photographs by the Author. All other photographs from the Authors collection unless otherwise indicated.

A Photrack Local History Book
© 1993 J.A.M. Vaughan
ISBN 0 9522190 1 8

Published by: Photrack PO Box 1203, Goring-by-Sea, Worthing, West Sussex BN12 4XU
Production by: Rail Photoprints Temple Cloud, Near Bristol
Typeset & Printed by The Longdunn Press Ltd. Barton Manor, St Philips, Bristol

Introduction

Situated on the Coastal Plain in West Sussex some 3 miles west of Worthing, just over 13 miles west of Brighton and 16 miles east of Chichester are the 'villages' of Goring and Ferring. Both are located between the South Downs to the North and the English Channel to the South.

These adjoining villages both pre-date their much larger neighbour of Worthing. Then known as Garinges and Ferringes both villages featured prominently in the Domesday Book of AD 1086. In Horsfield's 1835 History of Sussex, Goring Parish extended to 2120 acres and Ferring to 1070 acres. There has since been a tinkering of boundaries.

To the north an old flint wall just to the east of Highdown Hill and just west of the famous 'Miller's Tomb' delineates the Goring/Ferring boundary. The boundary continues in a north/south direction and now forms the great divide between Worthing Borough Council and the Arun District Council. Connecting the villages in an east/west direction is the famous Goring Hall Drive which is lined with 150 year old Ilex trees.

Another feature which both of the Goring and Ferring communities continually try to preserve is 'The Goring Gap'. This expanse of land would perhaps in other areas cause a split between communities but in this case it binds them. Due to be developed in the 1930s the Goring Gap is regularly under threat as yet another speculator or developer comes-up with the latest plan to build on a precious few acres of green belt.

In strictness the word village can hardly be used. It could have been used legitimately for both Goring and Ferring until about 1935 when Goring's population was about 1500 and Ferring's about 1000. At the 1991 census Goring had a population of about 22,000 and Ferring over 4,000.

The popular Highdown Hill is within Ferring's boundaries and Goring residents must cross the boundary to visit. On the other hand Ferring has never had a railway station and Ferring residents must cross the Goring boundary to travel by train. The A259 coast road runs through both Parishes and the River Rife traverses Goring on its way from the South Downs around Durrington to the sea at Ferring. Both Parishes are severed in a north/south split by the 'Coastway' railway line.

Following Goring's absorbtion into the Worthing Borough in 1929 it quickly became overrun as a western suburb of Worthing. Roads were widened and many of the oldest cottages were demolished. On the other hand Ferring resisted change, at least at the centre of the village, although there was still significant pre-war development.

'Goring and Ferring Past and Present' attempts to record many of the changes which have occurred over the last 100 years. It is unfortunate that through centuries past the wonderful world of photography had not been invented thus depriving future generations of accurate records of the social and architectural scene. The camera has only been in popular use for a century and it was not really until the birth of the picture postcard that photographs of village scenes were in general circulation. In 1902 it was Britain which became the first country to divide the address side of the postcard to allow messages thus allowing photographic reproductions to appear on the other side. These early postcards are now quite valuable and bearing in mind the small population it is a wonder that any have survived.

This volume does not purport to be a definitive history of either Goring or Ferring. The excellent 1987 Goring and Highdown book by Rev. Frank Fox-Wilson, which I had the privilege to be associated with, must be regarded as the definitive Goring history. Little has ever been written about Ferring except for a delightful little booklet describing St Andrew's Church in the village by the Rev. Rex Paterson and Sir Charles Cawley, which was published in 1982, and occasional articles. It is rumoured that a comprehensive history of Ferring dealing with the years to 1900 may be published in 1993/94.

What this book does do is to make available photographs and postcards from a huge collection which it has been my pleasure to amass over many years. The selection within these pages has been made from some one thousand views of the two villages. I believe the collection to be unrivalled and it now includes the famous Haffenden Collection which was acquired in 1991. One of the most fascinating aspects of preparing the book has been taking photographs which show the contemporary scene, in many cases from virtually the same location, as the old postcards.

One other objective of this publication is to show not just photographs from Edwardian times, interesting though such views are, but to also include scenes from the subsequent decades which have a fascination all of their own. As the years go by even the 1993 photographs will show unrepeatable views of 'village' life as it was at that time. While this book does not ignore the history of the villages the primary focus is on the 20th century rather than the Bronze Age, Iron Age, or Roman occupation. For many it is easier to relate to modern history, indeed for many older readers it will be the memory jerking scenes that will hold the attraction while younger readers will hopefully be fascinated to see 'how it was'. Also the last hundred years have of course seen the greatest period of change since the beginnings of mankind.

This book could not have been produced without the help and assistance of various individuals and organisations. In no particular order I would like to place on record the help of the Reverend Frank Fox-Wilson, Worthing Library Service, Borough Engineer's Office, Seeboard, Keith Smith, Christine Ada Smith, Audrey Bird, Keith Freak, Frank Grout, Terry Child, Nelson 'Haff' Haffenden, Ferring Library Service, Del Mercer and John Chalcraft. Thanks also go to the Worthing Herald, Worthing Gazette, West Sussex Gazette and the Evening Argus.

The production has been produced to the highest standards using top quality art paper because the exercise cannot be repeated without considerable repetition and there is little point spoiling the ship for a half penny worth of tar! It is my sincere wish that you enjoy 'Goring and Ferring Past and Present' and I hope it finds a place in every home where there is an intelligent interest in our local communities and their social history.

John A.M. Vaughan
Goring-by-Sea
September 1993

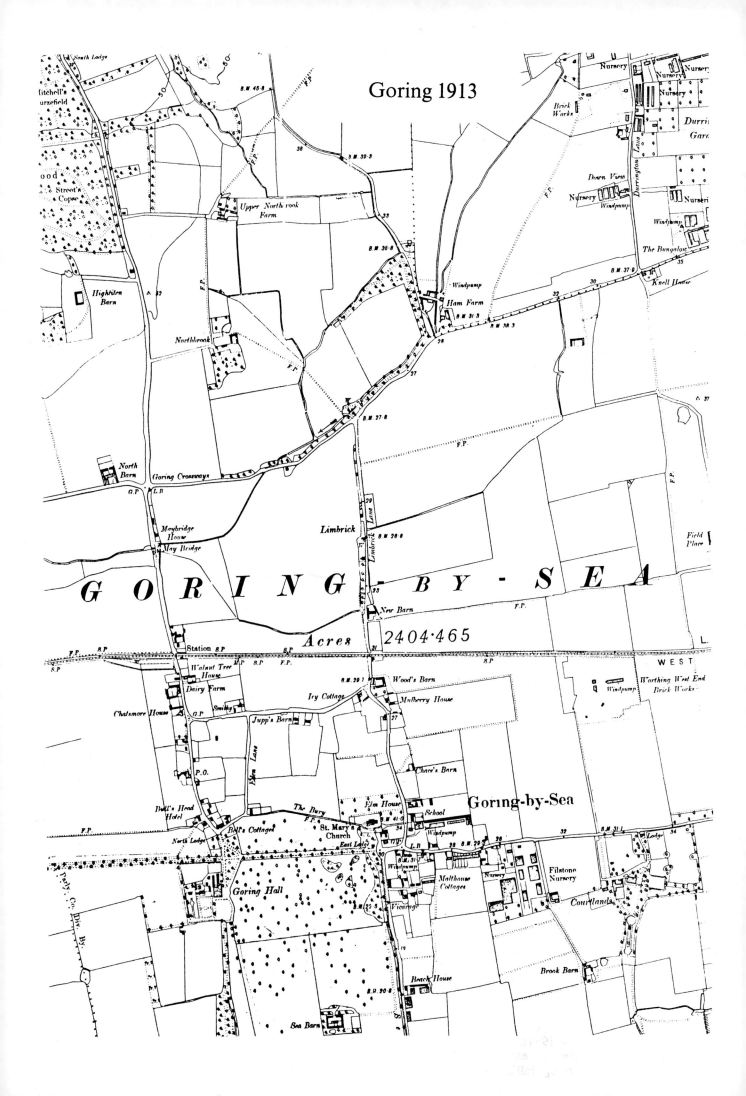

Goring 1913

GORING-BY-SEA

It is possible to trace the history of Goring back to ancient times but as is often the case it is the milestone of AD 1066 which provides a useful baseline or springboard from which to leap. At that time a number of manors made up the area known as 'Garinges' and it is a settlement of that name which features in the nationwide inventory of AD 1086 known as the Domesday Book which provides some early detail.

While not wanting to gloss over many hundreds of years it is a fact that although the large estates changed hands from time to time little else changed until the mid 19th century. There is ample evidence from surveys and from ecclesiastical records that for hundreds of years the population of Goring was static.

There was little immigration or emigration before the 19th century and the numbers required to farm land in a largely agricultural community did not vary. Mortality rates were high resulting in a stable rather than growing population. There was extreme poverty and without roads or railways transportation lent itself only to very local journeys, other than for the gentry. In fact a population of 419 in 1801 climbed to a mere 551 in 1901. Even by 1921 Goring residents totalled a modest 653.

Other than for the grandest buildings most structures before the middle ages were flimsy and made of little more than wattle and daub with straw roofs. Consequently although a building or two from that period survives most old buildings in Goring date back a mere 100 to 150 years. Sadly Goring has suffered badly from the failure of past Worthing Councils to have a strategy to save old buildings for posterity and demolitions over the past 50 years have been thoughtless in the extreme.

In terms of the major homes of Goring's past aristocrats the position is not as bleak and although modified over the years Field Place, Courtlands, Goring Hall and Castle Goring still survive. The only other 'high spots' are Tudor Cottage in the Goring Road, a few houses in the Jefferies Lane area, the Court House, the Old Cottage in Goring Way, Northbrook Farm House, the Bull Inn and a handful of flint barns which reflect the very early days. There are a few more survivors from the last century such as the Railway Station, the Goring Hall North Lodge, Beach House and the Limbrick Crossing building but overall the situation is grim.

The original village had its main centre around St Mary's Church with another sprinkling of buildings between the Bull Inn and the Railway Station. There were a few farms and cottages between the two on the alignment of Mulberry Lane, Jupps Lane and Goring Way. The village was connected to the Littlehampton Road by north/south roads of Limbrick Lane and Goring Street. The main route to Worthing was down a narrow Goring Lane, now the Goring Road. Other than for the private Goring Hall Drive and the Bury Footpath, the Littlehampton Road was the only public road between Goring and Ferring.

The arrival of the railway in 1846 had enormous impact and really put Goring on the map, although its impact was not immediate. There is no doubt that it was the decision to join the Borough of Worthing in 1929 which had the greatest impact on the village. Housing development had already spread out from Worthing to West Worthing and Goring was the developer's next target. Farms and nurseries were sold off at large profits and the arrival of the motor car and the omnibus all facilitated the changes of the 1930s.

Development enveloped the Sea Place area and Durrington-on-Sea station opened in July 1937. The Goring Lane was widened in 1934 and Jupps Lane bypass was completed in 1938. Development in the Sea Lane area started in 1937 after the Goring Hall Estate lands had been sold off. Houses around Ardingly Drive also started to spring up. In 1936 a new sewerage system was ready for service. From a population of 1389 in 1931 it had reached 11982 by 1951 and twice that figure by 1981.

The Goring Parish boundary has changed over the years and part of the old Parish has now become part of Maybridge Parish. In broad terms the western side of George V Avenue from the sea to the railway line forms the eastern boundary. The railway line itself but including the Sixth Form College forms another boundary as far as Goring Street, with a north/south Goring Street/Titnore Road line forming another boundary as far as the Arundel Road A27. The western boundary with Ferring is virtually a north/south line from the Arundel Road to the sea via the Miller's Tomb on Highdown Hill, across the railway line and Goring Way and down through the middle of the Goring Gap. The scope of this book includes parts of the original Parish and adjacent items of interest.

As the 21st century approaches Goring is still pleasantly residential and most would accept that there are far worse places to live. Residents have little distance to travel to reach either the Downs or the Sea. There are many pleasant areas to ramble including the greensward, the Plantation, Goring Hall Drive with its Ilex trees and the Highdown area. There are a number of sports grounds and recreational facilities. There is a rich choice of places to worship for those who feel so inclined. Public transport is reasonable and the Capital is just $1\frac{1}{2}$ hours away by train. There are plenty of local shops and Worthing is less than 3 miles distant. Schools are good quality and there are also colleges within the Parish. The 'pubs to population' ratio is on the low side. There is a thriving industrial estate and some large office complexes.

There have been numerous plans for change and development which have caused anxiety over the years. The Goring Gap is constantly under attack, there have been debates over the now completed bridge over the railway at Goring Station, the future use and access to Goring Hall, a waste tip proposal for delightful woodland just off of Titnore Road, the closure of Westholme old folks home, further development encroaching on the Highdown area, plans for traffic calming road humps and many many others. There is a delicate balance between beauty and disfigurement, progression and regression, good and bad.

Traffic growth is having an enormous impact and peak hour road congestion is becoming serious. Goring has not been able to avoid the national trends in crime rates with burglaries at record levels. Grass verges are no longer well maintained and so called 'travellers' regularly invade the sea front. Fortunately there are a large number of pressure groups in existence to oversee unwelcome developments and to prevent the unacceptable side of society from doing anything anti-social. The Goring Residents Association has over 2000 members and there are special interest groups such as the Ilex Group. There are also other social groups including, for example, the Womens Institute.

The photographs which follow and the information contained in the captions show the transition from yokel village to busy suburb over a period of about 100 years. No decade has been overlooked. Where there is impact, views have been shown in 'before and after' format although today's 'afters' quickly become tomorrow's 'befores'! The order starts to the north at Castle Goring and travels down to the Littlehampton Road and Highdown. The 'tour' then heads south from Goring Crossways via the Railway Station to the Bull Inn and Goring Hall. An amble down Goring Way and Mulberry Lane takes us to Mulberry Corner, the Church, Sea Lane to the sea. The journey continues along the Goring Road to West Worthing with a final glimpse over Durrington Bridge. I hope you enjoy the trip!

Castle Goring

Goring Castle,   Sussex,

Plate 3. Castle Goring is in fact just outside of the Goring Parish boundary. The building dates back to 1790 when Sir Bysshe Shelley, the Grandfather of the poet, commenced construction just south of the Worthing to Arundel road. Progress seems to have been patchy and by 1819 it was still in an unfinished state. It was finally leased to Captain George Pechell in 1825. This early view shows the southern Palladian aspect.

Plate 4. The northern 'half' of the Grade 1 listed Castle Goring was built in a Neo-Gothic style with due influence from Arundel Castle. The architect was Biagio Rebecca. In 1845 the property was purchased outright by the tenant (by then) Admiral Sir George Pechell R.N., for £11,250. The Castle Goring estate includes a huge area of woodland and farmland including Goring Woods and land in Clapham and Durrington. It was subsequently owned by the influential Burell and Somerset families. The building is now used as an International Cultural College and language school for foreign students.

CASTLE GORING. 1853

Plate 5. This tranquil scene was recorded on a postcard sent from Worthing in 1909. It shows a horse and cart paused on the hill at Castle Brow just outside of Castle Goring on what is now the A27 road. The mud on the road was common at that time due to poor or non-existent drainage. The motor car age was not then upon us!

CASTLE BROW,   GORING BY SEA.

Plate 6. The same scene some 84 years later with traffic moving quickly and in some volume along a dual carriageway. The variety of some of the trees on the left is common to both pictures. This underlines the conflict highlighted in this book between returning to the peaceful 'good old days' on the one hand while wanting good fast and safe roads on the other.

Plate 7. Goring has always had a fine scouting tradition. In Edwardian times the prospect of lengthy travels to go camping was remote and camps were normally set-up within cycling or walking distance. In this faded view Goring Scouts are at the camp grounds north of the Arundel Road on Easter Monday 1911. A Scout Hall, known as the Marriott Hall, was opened next to St Mary's Church in 1958.

Plate 8. The Somerset family have traditions in the Goring area going back over 100 years. Being in the upper echelons of the social scene they regularly received guests at Castle Goring such as Prince Ranji in November 1907. Paul Schweder of Courtlands is also in the group. In this view of Goring Woods a hunting party has been formed with participants sporting 12 bore shotguns and a good selection of hats but little game! A gamekeeper patrolled the woods and tried to make sure that the discouragement of poachers resulted in a good 'bag' but on this day perhaps the rabbits and pheasants kept their heads down.

Plate 9. Even during the author's lifetime the rural Titnore Lane was an attractive place for a stroll but in its post-1961 re-aligned form it has provided a vital link between the A27 and the A259 and consequently is much used by vehicular traffic. This 'S' bend around the gamekeeper's cottage can still be recognised and the building survives.

Plate 10. There have been farms at both Northbrook and Lower Northbrook for many centuries. The local Manor House once stood at 'North Brook' but was demolished by David Lyon when he built Goring Hall in 1840. A new farmhouse was built in 1852 and despite the encroaching housing estates of Durrington the building survives. The attractive flint building is seen here in 1986 (see also Plate 17).

Goring Cross Roads

Goring Cross Roads. 84.

Plate 11. At the junction of the present Littlehampton Road and Titnore Lane stood Goring Cross Roads (Crossways). The diminutive thatched cottage was once an old toll house and has featured in over two dozen different postcards of old Goring. This view from the north shows the postbox which was built-into the wall of the cottage.

Plate 12. The old postcard showing a horse and trap emerging from Titnore Lane into the Littlehampton Road at Goring Cross Roads was sent by Sam Haffenden Jr, son of the village blacksmith, to Miss Greenyer at Chesswood Road, Worthing on 30 June 1906. Northbrook College now stands on the corner to the right of the carriage.

GORING CROSS ROADS. — 2096

51 Goring Cross Roads looking East, Worthing.

Plate 13. This charming scene shows the Goring Cross Roads cottage from the west. The cross roads sign shows Goring and the Sea to the right, Clapham and Patching to the left, Worthing straight on and Littlehampton behind the photographer. Most of the trees in the area were elm trees and during the Second World War white bands were painted on their trunks due to restrictions on car headlights.

Plate 14. The mass destruction of Goring's old buildings started in earnest during the 1930s. One of the casualties was the famous Crossways Cottage. This photograph was taken on the 29 August 1938 and shows a Lake Bros. Ltd. lorry assisting in the demolition process. Most of the cottage's roof has just been removed. Note the company telephone number – Worthing 74!

Plate 15. Although most of Goring's old cottages have been swept away a number of flint barns have survived the passage of time. At the foot of the eastern slope of Highdown Hill is Hightiten Barn, seen here in December 1986. The Highdown Hill copse can be seen above right but this was all but destroyed in the 1987 hurricane.

Plate 16. Very near to the Northbrook 1852 farmhouse but located on the corner of Titnore Lane and Titnore Way is this fine flint and brick residence called simply 'The Cottage'. In the first published County Map of 1806 a building in approximately this location is shown although it is difficult to date precisely. The preservation of such buildings is invaluable unless we are to lose all trace of our local past.

Plate 17. An impressive survivor from a time when only farms occupied the area of land between the railway and the Arundel Road, west of Durrington village. This shows a fine flint barn adjacent to the farmhouse at (upper) Northbrook. Note particularly the characteristic windows and the large double doors. In the background the march of the housing estates continue it's relentless progress.

Plate 18. This casual stroller would be flattened within a matter of minutes if he attempted this walk up Titnore Lane today, especially on a Sunday when a regular car boot sale is held at Northbrook College. The straw covered road adds to the rural atmosphere. At the moment housing development has thankfully stopped at the eastern side of the lane.

Plate 19. Although this very old postcard view is rather dark it is unusual in showing the less familiar east to west view of Goring Cross Roads and affords the opportunity for a 'before and after' comparison. The focal point is the roofline of North Barn on the right, located on the north side of the Littlehampton Road.

Plate 20. Traffic had become so heavy that a footbridge was constructed across the Littlehampton Road, just to the east of Goring Cross Roads in the mid 1980s. In a comparison with the above photograph the prominent North Barn can be identified. Highdown Hill can be seen, above right (north west).

Nr. Worthing. *Northbrook Park Lodge, Goring.*

Plate 21. Another notable cottage, if anything smaller than Goring Crossways, was the picturesque Northbrook Park Lodge. The lodge was located just to the north of Limbrick Lane, near to the Sussex Yeoman pub and restaurant. It was the entrance to Northbrook Farm and may in olden days have been the southerly entrance to the old Manor House. It too was demolished in the 1930s. This view was taken from a postcard posted as early as 1904 so the original photograph was probably taken around the turn of the century.

Plate 22. Today the site of the former Northbrook Park Lodge is covered by the large Yeoman roundabout and the modern Toyota car showroom and offices, just opposite the equally new Southern Water Headquarters building. Again the dilemma between old world charm and commercial progress and jobs comes sharply into focus.

Plate 23. Not all changes relate to the turn of the century or even pre-war times. Changes are occurring daily and the significance is not always appreciated. This photograph overlooking what is now the Yeoman roundabout shows the scene in 1964, before the development of the Littlehampton Road. A mini car heads off for either Limbrick Lane or Palatine Road while another car trundles down the Littlehampton Road towards Ferring. Yeoman Road has yet to be driven through to Durrington.

Plate 24. Backing onto the sports ground visible in the above photograph is the Sussex Yeoman Country Carvery. The establishment was built to serve a growing community in the 1970s. Features such as a facsimile gas lamp, white posts and weather-vane result in an attractive appearance even though the building is modern.

WORTHING.—Littlehampton Road.—2097

Plate 25. This postcard was posted in 1909 and the message reads in part 'this is just one of the pretty roads around here.' It would be interesting to see if the writer could see anything pretty in the picture below. The cart is heading towards Goring Cross Roads, Limbrick Lane is on the left and Northbrook Lodge is behind the railings on the right.

Plate 26. The same view in 1993 finds a busy dual carriageway – Littlehampton Road, tall street lights, plenty of cars and a multi-storey office block – plus road works. The works were necessary to construct a new colour light controlled pedestrian crossing for the legions of new inhabitants to use, including many school children and students.

Plate 27. Until about 1965 the western end of the Littlehampton Road, within the boundaries of the Goring Parish, was a fairly quiet affair. When photographed in 1963 there was not even a white line down the centre of the road. There were still trees in abundance especially around the Highdown Gatehouses, visible on the left.

Plate 28. This 1993 photograph was taken with considerable risk to life and limb! Waiting for a gap in the traffic took some 10 minutes. The road is now dual carriageway with an unrestricted speed limit. All crossing points to Highdown Hill and into Ferring have been sealed off in the interests of safety, much to the understandable annoyance of Ferring residents who feel disadvantaged by these arrangements. The County Highways Committee has alledgedly failed to construct a roundabout at Langbury Lane, despite assurances.

Plate 29. The two Lodge Houses at the entrance drive to Highdown Towers were constructed in 1860. According to Lady Stern the main Littlehampton Road was a narrow lane sunk between high hedges and planted with ancient elms. This photograph was taken in December 1986 and since then both of the mature trees seen here have been felled.

Plate 30. The contents of Highdown Towers were sold in 1972 after Lady Stern's death for £70,000. The net value of her estate was £235,000. Although the interior fabric has been largely spoiled there are still attractions to be seen such as this former carriage house. In 1930 there were proposals to convert Highdown Hill into a golf course.

Plate 31. The famous Miller's Tomb has been a tourist attraction for some two centuries. Born in 1709 John Olliver came from Lancing where he worked the old post mill. In 1750 he took over Highdown Mill from his father Clement Olliver. He started to build his grave in 1765 at the age of 56. The eccentric miller kept his coffin under his bed and he was keen to show his neighbours how swiftly it could be removed by virtue of the wheels fitted to its base! The Miller died in 1793 aged 84. During 1981 some mindless vandals repeatedly drove a van into the grave and wrecked it. It has since been lovingly restored by craftsmen.

Millers Tomb and Highdown

Highdown Hill with an elevation of 269 feet has for centuries had an important influence in the history of both Goring and Ferring. This influence started some 10,000 years ago when Highdown is first thought to have become a settlement. This would have been the period of the Middle Stone Age. The oldest remains discovered in the Goring area date back to the New Stone Age around 3000 BC. Predictably these artifacts comprise flints and primitive tools.

Highdown Hill became a permanent settlement in the Old Bronze Age from around 2500 BC and several examples of pottery from that era have been found. The hill's inhabitants lived in simple circular huts and their encampments were protected by a simple ditch. The heavier earthworks visible today started life in the Iron Age when a fort was built around 500 BC. Several items in everyday use such as household objects, tools and crude jewellery relating to both Bronze and Iron Ages have been found on and around the hill and Worthing Museum has many fine items on display.

The Romans had an enormous influence throughout the land and there is ample evidence of their occupation in the Goring and Ferring areas. From AD 43 they brought with them organisation, administration, roads, law and order and slavery. In 1937 there were extensive excavations on the western slopes of Highdown when a Roman Bath-house was discovered. Even in those days the ruins were attacked by vandals! There have been Roman 'finds' near Goring Library, Compton Avenue, Bury Drive, Northbrook College and on Highdown Hill but the most significant find was the Goring Coin Hoard discovered in 1907 on land near Woods Way Industrial Estate. A pot containing 432 coins from around AD 280 was found. There are a number of old chalk pits in the area of Highdown.

When Mr Henty of Ferring Grange decided in 1892 to plant trees on the top of Highdown Hill a Saxon Cemetery was unearthed. Excavations produced evidence of over one hundred burials and many other cremations. The graves dated back to the 5th and 6th centuries. These pagans had some of their possessions buried with them and this produced something of a bonanza for archeologists.

Between the 6th and 8th centuries AD there is evidence that Christianity became a strong influence and around AD 800 it seems that a small church may have been constructed between Highdown Hill and the sea, in the area of St Mary's Church in Goring. Documentation in the form of charters and land grants suggest some order was again coming to the local community. Both Goring and Ferring get a mention in the Domesday Book and after the Norman invasion it seems that major landowners controlled what had become a rural agricultural community. There were few inhabitants living on Highdown Hill in the troubled Middle Ages. There had been a windmill on Highdown since 1587 (and probably before) but the mill once worked by John Olliver was finally demolished in 1826, 33 years after the famous miller's death (see Plate 31).

About 1820 the influential Lyon family built Highdown Towers on the south facing slope of the hill within the Parish of Goring. The house was the home of the Stern family for over 60 years. Sir Frederick Stern, botanist and Vice-President of the Royal Horticultural Society, created a 40 acre chalk garden on Highdown and he imported plants from all parts of the world (see Plate 2).

The famous ring of trees at the top of Highdown Hill was all but flattered by the 1987 hurricane and it has since been decided not to replace them because the roots might damage the ancient burial grounds. The Hill was acquired by the National Trust in 1938, and a spacious car park is well patronised by visitors to both Hill and gardens.

Plate 32. While cattle no longer graze around the Miller's Tomb walkers and their dogs can still find relative peace and take the time for a brief chat, as seen in this 1993 photograph. The old flint wall behind the tomb designates the Goring/Ferring boundary and although much of it is now covered by ivy and undergrowth, part has been restored due to the generosity of the late Edwin Pitches. The tomb was covered by Olliver's own somewhat melancholy poetry.

Lightning Strikes

LIGHTNING FATALITY AT GORING, SUSSEX.

Two young men named Sidney Charles Orchard, and Frederick Bennett Wadey, were killed when standing beneath this tree on Sunday afternoon, June 9th, 1907.

Plate 33. It seems that the months of June 1907 and 1908 brought some fierce thunderstorms to the Goring area. On 9 June 1907 four farm workers were caught in a storm and they chose to shelter under a large elm tree at the entrance to Highdown Towers, just a few yards from the Lodge Houses. Two young men, Sydney Orchard aged 19 and Frederick Wadey aged 22 were both killed when lightning struck the tree, another was injured and the fourth man was stunned. There was of course no radio or television and local entrepreneurs produced postcards of the incident. This superb postcard showing the tree and the east lodge, which is still extant, was posted on 25 June 1907 – 16 days after the event.

Plate 34. Postcards of the Orchard/Wadey incident included scenes at the burial and of the tombstone. However the most morbid card had to be this view of the horse drawn hearse leaving the Bull (formerly Bull's Head) Inn. The old Tap Room was regularly used as a mortuary because the thick walls resulted in a cool room. Inquests were also held at the pub. There are only two known examples of this postcard; the other being very battered. The grave can still be seen in Goring Churchyard.

Plate 35. Just one year later on the 4 June 1908 lightning again struck in the Goring area. Fortunately on this occasion it was only property which was damaged. A lightning bolt struck the village blacksmith's cottage which was located near Steele's Garage in Goring Way (see Plates 95 and 99). The strike caused the thatched roof to catch fire. In this photograph ladders are being used to affix a tarpaulin to the roof to keep the elements at bay pending repair.

Plate 36. In this unique photograph the interior damage caused by the lightning strike can be seen. Ornaments on the mantelpiece and a picture or mirror above the fireplace have been smashed, the wall covering has come away and there is evidence of severe scorching in the corner of the lounge. Of incidental interest is the ornamental fire surround, protective rail and gleaming poker and tongs.

Goring, Sussex.

Plate 37. At one time numerous streams crossed Goring on their way from the Downs to the sea. The River Rife still crosses the Parish. In order to cross the May stream and the Rife, May Bridge was built in the 19th century. May Bridge is located between Goring Cross Roads and Goring station. It gave its name to the post-war Maybridge Estate development. In this 1902 view two yokels lean against the flint wall of May Bridge. May Bridge House which was demolished in the 1970s can be seen in the right background.

Plate 38. This spectacular photograph (at least for bus enthusiasts!) shows a Southdown route '31' bus bound for Brighton crossing May Bridge in 1934. The bus is an open top Tilling Stevens model, registration UF 752. At this time the old Goring Street was about to be changed out of all recognition by road widening.

MAYBRIDGE, GORING, MAY 15-1935. 2

Plate 39. Pictured on 15 May 1935 the old May Bridge had been swept away and a new section of concrete road replaced the narrow track. From this time there was no longer a 'hump' in the road due to relevelling. North Barn can be seen on the left. The Strand was not then in the town planners mind and the nearest road to the east was Limbrick Lane.

May Bridge

Plate 40. Despite the extensive works of the mid-1930s the May Stream and River Rife were still susceptable to flooding in winter. In this view dated 21 March 1947 an Austin 10 car splashes its way towards May Bridge House and Goring Cross Roads. Note the short section of dual carriageway just beyond the road sign.

Plate 41. The same location in 1993 shows the customary increase in road traffic and the inter-section with the Strand (right). Modern flats have been built on the May Bridge House site but both Hightiten and North Barns are still standing. In the foreground the road has been re-aligned as part of the Goring railway overbridge development. Planning permission for the 77 acre Goring Green Estate was given in 1962. A total of 720 dwellings were built between Limbrick Lane and Goring Street.

Plate 42. Goring railway crossing looking south circa 1928. The 1900 signalbox can be seen on the right and the footbridge of similar vintage is equally prominent. At least four oil lamps can be seen and the mechanically operated crossing gates. These gates were to become the source of much delay to road traffic in later years.

Plate 43. During the First World War the land to the north of the railway line was used as an airfield by the Royal Flying Corps. The land to the west of Goring Street was used for army exercises. This army band is seen marching into the station forecourt on the north side of the line. The photograph was undated but just visible in the background are two new light-coloured electricity pylons. Seeboard were kind enough to confirm that the power lines at this location were installed in 1932.

Plate 44. This view of the crossing gates dates back to about 1905. The gate stop locking lever can be seen in the foreground while top right can be seen the London, Brighton and South Coast Railway lower quadrant semaphore starting signal. These gates were replaced by automatic barriers in 1985. Note the waistcoats worn by three of the permanent way staff.

Goring Railway Station

With the demolition of so many old cottages Goring station has become one of the most valuable survivors in the district. The railway came to Goring in March 1846 when an extension from Worthing to Lyminster was opened by the Brighton and Chichester Railway. This was absorbed by the London, Brighton and South Coast Railway in July 1846. The contractors were Messrs Hale and Wythes and construction progress across largely level ground was swift.

The line was built to double track specification, although initially only single track was laid. There was originally a small signalbox at the end of the down (westbound) platform and no footbridge. The crossing gates were hand operated. It may surprise readers to know that due to a recession the station was closed between November 1847 and June 1849!

Traffic grew and the second track was installed. In 1889 the Worthing Gazette reported that a new goods siding was one of many improvements being made by the railway at Goring. This would be welcome by local farmers and residents. At that time the nearest goods yards were at Worthing and Angmering. Corn, coal, manures and many other goods would be received and despatched. The goods yard opened in 1890.

In 1900 there were major changes as a new signalbox on the north west side of the crossing was opened, an overbridge was built and shortly afterwards the original station was extended. The signalbox had a Saxby and Farmer frame and it survived until 1988. All signals are now controlled from Lancing.

The line was electrified from 3 July 1938 and this undoubtedly contributed to the growth of Goring as a base for short and long distance commuters. Services increased over the years from four trains in each direction per day in 1853 to three trains per hour in each direction today.

The railway was the cause of a name change for the entire village of Goring on 6 July 1908. Confusion between Goring, Sussex and Goring (on Thames), Oxfordshire resulted in the village being called Goring-by-Sea from that date. This was reflected in Post Office cancelling handstamps being changed from the same date because letters and telegrams also went astray.

The story of Goring station could fill a book in its own right but mention must be made of the late Harry Ratley. He joined the platform staff at Goring-by-Sea in 1917 and finally retired in 1975 after 58 years of loyal service. The efforts of Harry Ratley, supported by Charlie Challen, Ray Wheeler and Ken Bond resulted in Goring winning the Best Kept Station award in 1957, 1958, 1959 and 1961.

Plate 45. The station sign proclaiming the name 'Goring' shows this to be a pre-1908 photograph. Evidence of the station extension is delineated by the new slates on the roof. On the right is the old lamp room where the paraffin to light the station and signal lamps was kept. The outbuilding survives, although in 1993 it was part covered in paint to cover graffiti applied by schoolchildren. An awning was added to the up side building in 1958.

Plate 46. Goring was honoured by the London and Brighton Company when they named a Class D2 0–4–2 tank locomotive 'Goring'. For some years the engine was allocated to the depot at Tunbridge Wells West. The locomotive is seen here taking on water with its No. 272 number plate gleaming in true 'Brighton' style.

Plate 47. Photographs of Goring station goods yard in operation are difficult to come by. This busy scene (courtesy of Frank Grout) was undated but research showed the lorry registration number PO 4660 on the left to be registered in July 1931. At least four lorries are in operation in this approximately 1937 picture. The goods yard finally closed during 1962.

Plate 48. This is the classic view from Goring footbridge. On Sunday 2 October 1932 former London & South Western Railway T9 Class 4–4–0 No. 725 speeds through with the 11.00 Portsmouth Harbour to Brighton express. The signalman keeps an eye on the five coach train. The goods yard can be seen on the left. The cameraman was the late Mr Madgwick who specialised in LBCSR lines.

Plate 49. Just prior to being diverted via the new Goring Green estate the Route 107 Southdown service is seen approaching Goring crossing in August 1966. The Leyland bus is passing a bus stop, the post of which can still be found in the undergrowth. The destination blind has plenty of local interest including Ferring (Henty Arms), North Ferring Corner and Goring Station.

Plate 50. An enthusiastic welcome from the Goring villagers awaited Mr and Mrs WFH Lyon on 5 February 1907. This was their first visit to Goring since their then recent marriage. Both the Goring Brass Band under Mr Frank Greenyer and the Vicar's Drum and Fife Band under Mr Frederick Greenyer were in attendance and they both struck up 'For He's a Jolly Good Fellow' following speeches. The couple travelled north to Castle Goring to spend some time with Mr and Mrs Somerset followed by a few days with Mr Edwin Henty at Ferring Grange. The Reverend Leefe is on the left.

Plate 51. In 1907 Railmotor coaches hauled or propelled by Class A1X 0–6–0 tank locomotives were extended in operation from Worthing to Littlehampton. In this gem of a photograph No. 663 prepares to leave Goring with an up train. On the right is the station master's house which still stands and is in use as a residence.

Plate 52. The same scene over 85 years later with the latest in British Rail's technology, a Class 158 diesel-hydraulic Sprinter, passing Goring with the 11.55 Cardiff to Brighton service. The old station master's house is in the background, the concrete fence and the brick lamproom have been painted to cover graffiti. Note the contrast in station seats and the update in lighting.

Plate 53. This was the view south from Goring crossing in 1905. The bolt fastener demonstrates that at this time the gates were opened manually. Walnut Tree Farm is on the left and Railway Cottages are in the central background. The lady and child pose opposite the new footbridge.

Plate 54. The southern extension to the footbridge was removed in 1985, the same year as the old crossing gates were replaced by automatic barriers. Railway Cottages have gone but the lower part of the old flint wall on the left is still in place. On weekdays the street is full of cars as few passengers are willing to pay BR's exhorbitant parking fees, currently £1.50 per day.

Plate 55. Goring station looking north west from the new road bridge. The foreground buildings were built on part of the old Walnut Tree Farm following the demolition of the latter. The station master's house is on the right. Behind that is the modern Mormon Church of Latter Day Saints. Fortunately the fields behind the station continue to be farmed providing the northern part of the 'Goring Gap' between Goring and Ferring.

Plate 56. This wonderfully rural aspect gives the correct impression that Goring-by-Sea railway station has always been a country station. From a population of 535 in 1861 Goring's population grew in 100 years to 18,791 in 1961. It now exceeds 22,000. This excellent Tuck & Co postcard shows the scene circa 1954.

GS 3   RAILWAY STATION AND HIGHDOWN, GORING BY SEA   A TUCK CARD

Plate 57. The same view as Plate 58 in March 1993 with the left hand station chimney as the only object common to both views. The crossing warning signs both have red triangles and a crossing gate symbol. The location of the posts in Goring Street are virtually the same but the removal of the cottages and the resulting straight road now give a clear view of the actual crossing.

Plate 58. Railway Cottages just south of the station were on the local authorities long demolition list. These ancient thatched dwellings had been allowed to deteriorate over the decades and by 1948 their fate had been determined. With the thatch in visibly poor condition the buildings await their fate. Their demolition enabled Goring Street to be straightened. Note the level crossing warning sign and the station in the right background.

Plate 59. A rare shot of Walnut Tree Cottage and Farm in January 1938. In the background above the flint wall is the new railway overbridge embankment which was started that year and which was completed exactly 50 years later! Finance and the Second World War both intervened. Above the embankment are the roofs of the then new houses in Ardingly Drive.

Plate 60. This photograph shows the Dairy Farm to the left and Railway Cottages to the right. Highdown Hill can be seen in the background. In 1931 Dairy Farm was occupied by Walter Burton who was the bailiff to George Harrison who lived in the adjacent Chatsmore House. Walnut Tree Farm was run by Roderick Hartcup, Dairy Farmer.

Plate 61. The same view as the previous plate photographed in March 1993. The old buildings have long gone but the old names have been preserved in the road Chatsmore Crescent and in the flats opposite called Dairy Farm. The site of Railway Cottages is occupied by one of the few commercial buildings in the area and the goods yard is now a second hand car lot.

Goring Street

The Village.   Goring.

Plate 62. This postcard was postally used in 1907. The photograph was taken at the junction of Goring Street and Jupps Lane (now Goring Way at this point). Looking north the buildings from left to right are Chatsmore House, Dairy Farm, Railway Cottages and Walnut Tree Farm. Local children keep an eye on the photographer and a motorised tricycle makes an interesting 'prop'.

Plate 63. The same scene today with the new Chatsmore House just visible and the Dairy Farm apartments in the centre of the picture. Set back from the road is Chatsmore Roman Catholic School which was first constructed in 1956 and later extended. Curiously a grassy triangle of land has survived giving an impression of open space.

Plate 64. Chatsmore House and Farm were located to the west of Goring Street with land extending down towards Singleton Crescent near the Ferring boundary. In this 1938 view the front of the house is covered in ivy with an uncharacteristic rendered wall. Goring Street was subjected to major drainage and widening works in 1938 and 1959.

Plate 65. As part of the suburbanisation of Goring, with building rapidly extending from east to west, Chatsmore House became superfluous to requirements and was demolished in 1962. Strange to relate that demolition was by fire as vividly illustrated in the photograph taken by Alex Lowe on 23 February 1962.

Plate 66. The new Chatsmore House apartment block. The building is pleasantly situated behind one of Goring's old flint walls and attractively framed by trees. An old style red telephone box was removed from this location in 1991 when less substantial modern boxes were installed at Goring Station and in Aldsworth Avenue.

Plate 67. 15 September 1938 is the date of this interesting view looking east along Jupps Lane (now Goring Way). The road behind the photographer leads to the Bull Inn while on the left is Goring Street leading to Goring station. On the right in front of the huge elm trees is the site of Aldsworth Avenue and in the background can just be seen Haffenden's Forge and adjacent thatched cottages. A sign advertises bungalows for sale for £795!

Plate 68. There seems to have been dramatic changes in this March 1993 photograph. While the alignment of the curb, right foreground, is recogniseable the only other focal point common to both views is the now white thatched cottage which is visible between the poles of the A259 road sign. In the background is Fads home decorations store and Steele's Garage, plus the Aldsworth roundabout. On the corner of Goring Street and Goring Way, now the site of Oakland Court, once stood the Goring and Ferring Evangelical Free Church.

Plate 69. Goring has at least for the last century had a fine cricketing tradition. Goring Cricket Club dates back to 1877 but there is evidence of cricket matches taking place in the Parish as long ago as 1812. Sir Frederick Stern challenged the Goring Team to a match annually with a team made up of men and boys from the East End of London who camped on Highdown in the summer months. In this 1912 scene villagers have dressed-up as a comic cricket team to celebrate the Coronation of King George V.

Plate 70. On the east side of Goring Street but south of Jupps Lane were Elm Tree Cottages and Laurel Cottage, seen here in a faded postcard of about 1905 vintage. Out of view on the left was Hempstead Cottage. Nos. 1 and 2 Elm Tree Cottages were demolished on 4 June 1969 and replaced by modern houses and flats.

Plate 71. Being a rural farming community it is perhaps not surprising that a relatively large number of photographs were taken at harvest time. In this well posed Edwardian scene Sunday School attendees and teachers all in their best Sunday dress pick up handfuls of hay for the photographer.

Plate 72. To help supplement their incomes many villagers opened their homes for the sale of afternoon teas. This part of Elm Tree Cottages (and the Blacksmith's Forge) was no exception; note the small sign in the window. The daughter of the family opens the gate as if to invite the photographer in for tea.

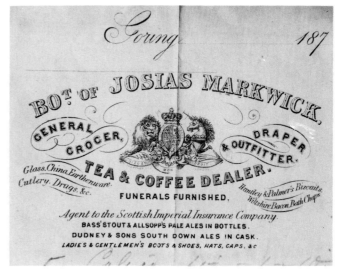

Plate 73. (Above, right) This piece of Goring stationery has survived since the 1870s and shows the remarkable diversity of activity at Markwick's store. Locals could buy a suit, purchase some Allsopp's ale, buy some aspirin or a glass as well as having their funeral furnished.

Plate 74. Markwick & Son's Store was located just north of the Goring cricket field which is adjacent to the Bull Inn. The shop first became the village Post Office in 1888 when Rupert Markwick's Mother opened a sub-post office in her store. Rupert took over in 1905. A significant development took place in 1910 when the first telephone switchboard in Goring was installed. In 1929 the Post Office transferred to a small shop in Mulberry Lane. Rupert who was a very competent cricketer died in 1956 at the age of 81.

Plate 75. The view looking south down Goring Street towards the Bull Inn and Moors Cottages. The old flint wall on the right survives and is the boundary of the Goring recreation and cricket ground. These mature trees were replaced many years ago. In the early days the field doubled as a cow pasture and it is said that the cricketers had to be careful when diving to stop a ball.

Plate 76. The same view today with only the flint wall and the pub surviving. The road was widened in 1959 but other significant changes took place in 1937/38. An old wooden pavilion at the north end of the 'Rec' was replaced by the present structure in the 1960s.

Plate 77. This postcard was sent from Goring to Brighton at 10 a.m. on 15 June 1912. It was taken from the front of the Bull Inn looking north up Goring Street. Behind the two locals can be seen Markwick's store, with horse and cart outside, as well as Rose and Magnolia Cottages in the distance.

Plate 78. The modern 1987 view was taken from the same place and shows that not a single original building has survived and only the dip in the flint wall in the foreground gives a common focal point.

Preservation

The cuttings on this page show just a handful of issues where the preservation of Goring was potentially at stake. There have been regular occurrences over the past 60 years where proposed changes and developments have needed careful analysis to determine whether they are in the interests of the community. Many battles have been lost but there have been some notable successes. What **IS** important is that the residents show an interest and care what happens to their environment. They should bring pressure to bear when changes are likely to be detrimental or reduce the quality of life.

County agrees to keep crossing

A 'BACKDOWN' by West Sussex County Council has meant a partial victory for Goring campaigner John Bristow.

Mr Bristow was preparing to take his battle to court. He was outraged the council had decided to close Goring level crossing now the new overbridge is open.

He said the elderly, disabled and cyclists would not be able to use the footbridge and would be forced to walk right round the busy overbridge.

But County Hall cancelled the court ~ planned for Wednesday and a new `~` place on April 19.

In court the council will apply to close the crossing to all motor vehicles — but a section near the station will be kept open for pedestrians, horse-riders and cyclists.

Mr Bristow said he saw the 'backdown' as a partial victory and meant the council was starting to see sense.

'I am still battling for the crossing to be open for emergency vehicles, because if there is an accident on the railway or the A259 then the ambulances will need to get through', he said.

Conservationists win fight over tip

A FIGHT to stop a massive rubbish tip being sited near a Worthing beauty spot has ended in victory.

Wimpey Waste Management's appeal against West Sussex County Council's refusal of permission for a landfill site, west of Titnore Lane, was blocked by the Department of the Environment last week.

The decision was warmly received by local conservation groups, which have been battling against the plans.

Worthing Green Party members described the news as a 'major environmental victory for local people'.

Spokeswoman Lucie Colkett said, 'Had the scheme gone ahead, the effects of litter, vermin, environmental destruction and increased traffic volumes would have been horrendous.

'The existing woodland provides a buffer between the A27 and the A259. Had it been turned into a rubbish tip with lorries thundering through, there would have been no relief from traffic noise and pollution. A quiet haven would have been destroyed.'

The group claims the tip conflicted with the Worthing Structure Plan, which seeks to restrain development likely to damage the landscape's character.

The party said the news brought hope that the DoE listened to objectors.

Jackie Young, former press officer for Worthing Friends of the Earth, said, 'The group is obviously delighted at the outcome of this inquiry as we did not believe the landfill should be allowed.'

Fight to save an old house

GORING HOUSEHOLDERS are banding together in an effort to save an old house.

Plans have been lodged to demolish Beach House at 64 Sea Lane and build 21 old folk's flats on the land — and this has made existing householders in the area see red.

Mr John Jewsbury, of Sandown Close, organised a protest meeting which was attended by about 50 people.

'The house is at least 100 years old and is an integral part of the road,' he said. 'It would ruin the look of the area to pull it down and build flats. Trees would be wrecked to make way for garages.'

Mr Jewsbury and his neighbours are now furiously writing letters to Worthing Borough Council planning committee in a bid to stop the developer in his tracks.

Worthing MP Terence Higgins has also been approached about the plan in order to gain his support.

The Bull Inn

Plate 79. The Bull Inn, seen here in June 1965, was originally called the Bull's Head Inn. It is thought to have been built in the reign of George II, although one source states 16th century and another more specific source pinpoints the year as 1770. There was limited modernisation in the early part of this century with further changes in recent times, when the old tap room was opened out (this room also doubled as a games room and even a mortuary on occasions) and the bar was moved from one side of the pub to the other. An extension was built in 1888 but until recent times this was not part of the public area. The pub has no coaching history because it was always well off the beaten track in main road terms, provision was however made for stabling. On the left hand side of the frontage was once a small butcher's shop but this is now part of the kitchen. There was a small hatch for 'off licence' sales. In an early advert it was described as 'a very popular halt for motorists, cyclists and ramblers, and provides a pleasant restful atmosphere for the enjoyment of fine Sussex ales and snacks'. The fine Tamplins Sussex ale was taken over by Watneys in 1953 who closed the Brewery in 1973, hardly 'fine Sussex ales'! At one time King and Barnes of Horsham provided a guest beer. The popular pub has won prizes for its gardens.

Plate 80. On the north eastern corner of what is now the junction of Goring Street and Fernhurst Drive stood Bell's Cottages, seen here. In 1931 the cottages housed six families with the surnames Patching, Attwater, Baker (i), Baker (ii), Greenyer and Gander. They were demolished after the Second World War but the exact date cannot be determined.

Plate 81. This is the same scene in 1993 with the only survivor being the distant flint wall, just to the right of the car. The wall forms the frontage of the Methodist Church on Bury Drive which was built in 1956. Just beyond the old Bell's Cottages a muddy wooded lane known as Eden Lane ran down to Jupp's Lane.

Plate 82. This fascinating view shows the three-home terrace known as Moors Cottages which was located next to the Bull Inn. In 1931 the family surnames were White, Dellman and Marley. In this Edwardian photograph only the ladies of the households and their children make an appearance; possibly the men were at work. The cottages look rather damp and their condition must have worstened because they too were swept away in the name of progress.

Plate 83. This is the only known photograph of the Goring Village Reading Room which was located directly opposite the Bull Inn next to Bell's Cottages. The brick edged flint building with tiled roof looks to be in excellent condition in the circa 1906 view. The Reading Room may have been a small library but it is known that it doubled as a village function room and The Women's Institute first met here in 1920. The children's clothes will please the students of social history.

Plate 84. The North Lodge of Goring Hall was a well used entrance; the alternatives being the long drive down through the Ilex trees bordering Goring Hall Drive. The building dates from about the time of the Goring Hall 1888 rebuild. Note particularly the ornate barge-boards, the tall chimneys and the gateposts.

Plate 85. As seen in this 1993 picture the Lodge has survived and presents a refreshing change to more modern homes in the vicinity. The decorative boarding has gone and the chimneys have been considerably shortened but the gateposts are still there, even though no longer used for vehicular access to Goring Hall. On the right Fernhurst Drive leading to Bodiam Avenue runs where Moors Cottages were sited.

Goring Hall antique raid

PROFESSIONAL thieves struck at Goring Hall School, in Ilex Way, Worthing, stripping out more than £20,000 worth of antique fireplaces.

The thieves forced a window at the rear of the unoccupied mansion and took 11 antique fireplaces, either removing them completely or painstakingly removing the Belgian tiles from them. An antique wash stand was also stolen.

The centrepiece fireplace with its huge oak surround, standing 10ft across and from the floor to ceiling was also taken out.

Police believe a team of professional builders were responsible, probably taking the fireplaces out over several days.

They want to hear from anyone who might have seen a team of men appearing like builders and with a large vehicle at Goring Hall betwen last Monday and Friday.

A police spokesman said: "These fireplaces are valuable with a market in this country and abroad. The fireplaces at Goring Hall were of exceptional quality."

Plate 86. David Lyon, a merchant who did much business with the West Indies bought the Goring Hall Estate in 1834. The manor house was then located at Northbrook. He demolished the building and built Goring Hall on a site just south of the Bull Inn in 1840. He was also instrumental in the demolition and rebuilding of St Mary's Church in 1837. The Hall was burnt to the ground in 1888 and a virtual replica was rebuilt on the same site. It was leased to the Molson family in 1906 before becoming a private school in the 1920s. This impression shows the Hall circa 1926. The Hall has links with the Queen Mothers Bowes-Lyon family.

Plate 87. There were extensive outbuildings in the grounds and many of these are original, pre-dating the rebuilt Hall. By 1988 the Hall had fallen out of use following the departure of the last student. Many of the students were the sons of foreign aristoctats. The Hall has gradually fallen into disrepair, a situation not helped by the theft of eleven huge Victorian fireplaces. After much local hassle with most residents wanting the Hall to be used as a hospital but not wanting the associated traffic or access problems, permission for its change of use was granted. This 1993 photograph shows a rather sad-looking Hall with all the ground floor windows boarded-up.

Plate 88. The foundation and approach ramps for a bridge over the railway at Goring were put in place in 1938, using much of the spoil removed from the Jupps Lane bypass work. An article in the Worthing Gazette in 1968 suggested that the bridge would be built 'when the money was available'. In this January 1986 scene the horse and pony grazers have erected a 'No To Bridge' protest notice, but work started shortly afterwards.

Plate 89. The main bridge spans over the railway line were positioned in November 1987 and the new £1 million road bridge was opened the following year. In this spring 1993 photograph the bridge had become well established carrying heavy volumes of traffic. The local authority have done a superb job in daffodil planting on Aldsworth roundabout.

GS 1   GORING WAY, GORING BY SEA   A TUCK CARD

Plate 90. Although Ardingly Drive was a pre-war development these bungalows along Goring Way were built post-war. Similar buildings appeared along the entire length of Goring Way beyond the Ferring boundary. This was testimony to the increase in the retired population who preferred bungalows for ease of maintenance and mobility. The concrete road replaced the old lane in 1938. A hedgerow has grown along the service road since this 1954 photograph was taken.

Plate 91. Residents of Goring about to leave the Bull Inn on a charabanc outing courtesy of Southdown Motor Services circa 1922. There are two dozen men visible but not a single lady. Perhaps this was a working mans or sports club outing. The picture was supplied by Mrs P Mesham.

Plate 92. The biggest mistake for the preservation of old Goring was its absorbtion by Worthing in 1929. Over the years Goring has been used to accommodate a suburban sprawl so that the village identity has been almost (but not entirely) lost. Some development must be expected and a growing community must live somewhere, but the growth itself has not been the problem it has been the wholesale demolition of Goring's heritage. In this 1936 photograph the old cottages at the top of Sea Lane are being demolished, including that of Mr Cecil Pescott, the village chimney sweep.

Plate 93. The lovely little Laburnum Cottage situated just north of the Conservative Club in Mulberry Lane was torn down on 3 September 1938 when the Jupp's Lane bypass work was going on. Except for its partially stripped thatched roof the dwelling looks to be in good condition.

Plate 94. The original crossing keeper's cottage at Limbrick Lane, is still standing but has lain derelict for many years. Will anybody take the trouble to save it? The crossing keeper here opened the gates across the railway line until the road was sealed-off and a pedestrian subway was built in the 1960s. The old flint part of the building probably dates back to the opening of the railway in 1846.

The tragedy of Goring

Plate 95. Arguably the greatest tragedy of recent times was the demolition of the old Haffenden cottage in 1966, when the author took this photograph. The building and the adjacent Forge had been a part of village life for a couple of centuries, now Steele's Garage covers part of the site. Surely it was not beyond the wit of man to have preserved the classic building? In 1966 the Chairman of the Worthing Town Planning Committee who had been considering the application by H D Steele and Son to extend their premises said 'This is private property. These cottages, although old, are not listed as houses of historical value'. Councillor Howard Watts went on to say that 'I like old cottages but I think in this instance they're a little out of place'. It was reported in the Evening Argus of 13 October 1966 that Alderman Horace Steele, owner of the garage, and a former Mayor of Worthing, was 'abroad at present' (and therefore not available to comment).

Plate 96. In 1872 the village blacksmith was one George Rowe but at about the turn of the century the smithy was taken over by the famous Haffenden family. In this 1907 postcard the family appear in front of the delightful cottage which was so hastily demolished in 1966. Young Sam Haffenden (Jr) was courting one of the Greenyer girls during the first decade of the century and he was a prolific writer of postcards to her. Thankfully many of these were preserved and were acquired by the author from the family in 1991.

Plate 97. Sam Haffenden made great use of his forge and he tried his hand at inventing on more than one occasion. With the two Sam Haffendens sitting on a tandem in front of the 17th century Goring Forge they seem to have found a novel way of carting Mother about the village. This splendid invention does not seem to have been repeated, and was presumably never patented.

Plate 98. A homely view of the Haffenden family circa 1910. With repairs to farm machines, shoeing horses and in later years servicing lawnmowers the family carved a living as blacksmiths for nearly 60 years. They also participated in most village activities and those of the local church.

The Forge

THE FORGE GORING-BY-SEA.

Plate 99. Once the Forge had been demolished the two thatched cottages were the next target. This early postcard shows the close proximity of the two dwellings. Fortunately the cottage on the right was not demolished and it now has the distinction of having the only thatched roof in Goring. In 1931 'The Cottage' (its actual name) was owned by Frederick Harrison.

Plate 100. The thatched roof of The Cottage was damaged in the 1987 hurricane and it has since been reroofed by a thatcher from Devon. In 1993 it looked to be much cared for and was in pristine condition with a coat of paint adding to the appeal of its leaded light windows. Steele's Garage can be seen on the left.

Plate 101. Jupp's Barn was near dereliction in September 1960 when seen through the lens of the camera of R J Downer. Having been a church meeting place for many years the Roman Catholic community acquired it in the mid 1960s and with the energies of Canon Westlake built an impressive extension to the structure in 1968. They achieved the perfect balance of saving an old flint building but tastefully adapting it for modern use.

Plate 102. A remarkable restoration for the old Jupp's Barn. With old windows modified and old brick and flint work repointed the new tiled roofed structure is in everyday use within and outwith the Catholic community. Recently, to the west of the barn, part of the Cistine Chapel has been reproduced. The highly acclaimed work now has a firm place on the sites of Goring list.

Plate 103. This Edwardian scene shows the Haffenden family outside of their cottage in about 1910. Goring was then a close-knit community with most villagers knowing each other. Everybody of course knew the village blacksmith and Sam Haffenden was verger and, from 1939, captain of the bell tower at St Mary's church.

Plate 104. Just down the lane was Ivy Farm where the Greenyer family lived. As previously mentioned the Greenyers ran the village bands for many years. In Victorian times some of the Greenyer cattle could be found grazing some distance from the farm which necessitated driving the cattle through the village. Mr Greenyer is third from the left in this picture, alleged to be in 1905 but I suspect somewhat later.

Plate 105. Wood's Cottages disappeared from the map before the Second World War. They were located on the bend in the road where Limbrick Lane joined Mulberry Lane and Jupp's Lane; on the eastern side. Wood's Barn was just behind the properties. The site is now occupied by the Woods Way Industrial Estate. Note the spire of St Mary's Church just visible on the right.

Plate 106. The remaining two layers of flint wall seen here could well be the only remains of the Wood's Cottages front garden boundary. One of the Woods Way factories can be seen on the left while the church spire can just be glimpsed to the left of the house, far right. Limbrick Crossing is behind the photographer in this 1993 illustration.

Mulberry Lane

Plate 107. The Goring Road was widened in 1934 and by 1938 it was the turn of the Mulberry Lane/Jupps Lane area. The new road ran from the telephone exchange in Mulberry Lane to Jupp's Barn, thereby avoiding the sharp corner by Ivy Farm. In this view, looking north towards the Conservative Club on the left, the new concrete alignment is being prepared with an elderly tipper truck depositing hardcore as a base. In the background is Laburnum Cottage, soon to be demolished (see Plate 93). Photographed in March 1938.

Plate 108. In this 1993 equivalent the Conservative Club is the only survivor. Dagenham Motors the local Ford dealer can be seen in the right background. In the 1950s this site was occupied by Eirene Garage which was always littered with pre-war 'bangers'. On the right is the junction with Barrington Road.

Plate 109. Many of the council houses in Barrington Road and associated roads are now in private hands. The houses were mostly built just after the 1939–1945 war and development continued until the late 1950s in the Palmerston Avenue area. The paving stones have now sunk slightly and the concrete road, now over 50 years old, shows sign of repair.

Plate 110. In 1938 only the kerbstones of Barrington Road had appeared. On the right can be seen Highdown Hill and in front of the Conservative Club stands a vintage steam road roller working on the Mulberry Lane improvements.

Plate 111. Frampton Court is a modern block of apartments which was built on the site of the old Council Cottages. The new accommodation was popular with senior citizens offering a combination of easy maintenance, no garden to manage and a degree of security. Yet again walls and gateways can be compared.

Plate 112. Council Cottages in Mulberry Lane were amongst the first council housing provided in the village of Goring. They stood on the eastern side of the lane next to the twitten leading up to Goring First School. They were demolished in July 1974 to make way for Frampton Court. The two signs read 'Danger Keep Out' and on the upstairs window 'Demolition by. . . .'

Plate 113. When Rupert Markwick transferred his Post Office from Goring Street to Mulberry Lane in 1929 he operated from a seven by twenty feet store (now a shoe repairers) next to this building. Early in December 1946 he served his last customer and retired at the age of 70. This new Post Office building opened the next day. The telephone exchange which also served Ferring was in an adjacent building. The '999' emergency facility was available from 1948. After 46 years of service the Post Office has now moved to Mulberry Parade in the Goring Road. The red telephone box has been removed since this December 1986 view.

Plate 114. Prior to the 1840s only the wealthy children in the village received any formal education but when Margaret Bushby died in 1840 she left £4000 for the education of 30 boys and 30 girls in Goring and Durrington. A school was completed and opened in 1844 with Mr George Buster as Headmaster. The school was located in Mulberry Lane. Average attendance in 1880 was 60 children. Here children gather round Mr Cartwright in a 1907 school photograph.

Plate 115. As the population grew the school became increasingly overcrowded. The school had very limited facilities with water in a bucket being the only washing place for children. By 1957 the building was in a shocking state of repair with half a dozen buckets in position to collect rain water and with the staff toilet frozen solid in Winter. A new school was planned and the old Dickensian building seen here in 1959 was demolished in the following year.

THE SCHOOL, MULBERRY LANE, GORING BY SEA

Plate 116. This view looking down Mulberry Lane towards the Parade dates from the late 1940s. The postcard was published by Wylder, the owner of the confectioners next to the Mulberry Bakery in the flat-topped building. The semi-detached dwelling beyond was demolished in the early 1970s. An Austin 12 and an Austin 7 are the only vehicles in sight.

Plate 117. The same view in 1993 with the Mulberry Bakery building and the school's front wall common to both plates. After demolition of the old school building the site was converted into a rose garden. A pedestrian crossing was installed opposite the twitten to the school in 1992, hence the 'zig-zag' lines in the foreground.

Plate 118. It's 1906 and school is out in Mulberry Lane. With no vehicular traffic whatsoever many of the youngsters are ambling in the middle of what is now a busy thoroughfare. The original postcard has Goring School marked with a cross. Note the 'stepped' flint wall and wattle fencing in front of the now demolished house on the right. Elm House is visible in the background.

Plate 119. The 'stepped' flint wall in Plate 118 is the only piece of infastructure to survive into 1993. When the above photograph was recorded Goring had just two oil street lights; one by the railway station and the other at the end of Jefferies Lane. Just after 1910 another dozen oil lamps were installed and Sam Haffenden Jr was the official lamplighter. Today numerous modern lights are extremely efficient at lighting the area.

Plate 120. The comment on the back of this 1909 card reads "This is a view of the old church we went to this morning. It is about five miles from here. They have a splendid vicar". The writer was referring to the Reverend George Leefe who held the post from 1901 until 1916. The hayfield is now covered by shops. To the right once stood Burrel Cottage.

THE CHURCH, GORING BY SEA.

Plate 121. A major development for the Goring community was the establishment of a public lending library in 1956. The new building was strategically placed just to the east of the Court House and the Church. Particular attention was given to the grounds which often sport a colourful array of flowers. New public toilets were built at the same time.

THE LIBRARY, GORING BY SEA, SUSSEX. 314

St Mary's Church

Plate 126. Although there is now a rich choice in places of worship in Goring, in terms of local tradition none can compete with the 'C of E' St Mary's Church. There is evidence of a place of worship on the present site dating back to Saxon times. The predecessor of the present church dates back to the 12th century with 14th century alterations. The old church was demolished in 1837 and rebuilt with funds provided by the Lyon family. Note the railings around the Lyon family grave in the background and by the footpath. Most were removed for the war effort around 1940. The spire was re-shingled in 1971.

Plate 127. This postcard of the inside of St Mary's shows the famous Feibusch Mural. The Bishop was keen to show the church as a patron of the arts but there was considerable opposition to the painting of the mural. Some of the figures were described as violently masculine and brutal. After much debate the mural received the green light and it was completed and dedicated in September 1954.

GORING CHURCH, GORING-BY-SEA.

ST. MARY'S, GORING-BY-SEA

Plate 128. This photograph was taken from the site of the Sea Lane roundabout looking eastward down the Goring Road. The 1936 scene shows Peacock Hall Hotel vacant and awaiting its inevitable fate. The nearby site of Peacock Hall Farm sported a high water tower. The site is now occupied by the Mulberry Hotel.

Plate 129. At the east end of Goring Hall Drive, now the east end of Ilex Way, there was a lodge house and huge decorative iron gates. Occupied by the Martin family in 1910 and by Mrs Batley in 1931 the lodge was demolished after the sale of the estate in the mid-1930s. The gates were scrapped for the war effort in 1940. This postcard dates back to 1906.

The Entrance Gates,   Goring Hall, Sussex.

Plate 130. Two ladies stand admiring the magnificent chestnut tree that still stands on the corner of Sea Lane and Ilex Way. No doubt to the irritation of the owners small boys have for generations tried to recover the 'conkers' by hurling objects up into the tree. The tasteful Goring Hall development started with Sea Lane in 1937/38.

ILEX WAY, GORING BY SEA, SUSSEX.

247

The Mulberry Hotel, Goring by-Sea. 2946.

Plate 131. The Mulberry Hotel replaced the Peacock Hall Hotel in 1938. The imposing building was designed to meet the growing needs of a largely middle class community who were gradually populating the Goring Hall Estate.

Plate 132. The old thatched cottages at the north end of Sea lane rival Goring Cross Roads Toll Cottage for the number of times featured on local postcards. They were certainly picturesque. In this timeless scene a smart horse and carriage pose for the camera just after the turn of the century. On the right is the six foot high flint wall which at one time ran around the entire perimeter of the lands belonging to Goring Hall.

1619 Sea Lane-Goring-Sussex

Sea Lane, Goring-by-Sea. 2146/1.

Plate 133. After the purchase of the Goring Hall Estate by Hesketh Estates Ltd the latter company were advertising their acquisition as '800 acres of sunshine'. The company started to lay out roads before the Second World War starting with Sea Lane and working south and west. Having swept away the old flint boundary wall these homes in Sea Lane were amongst the first to be built.

Plate 134. These Goring urchins are holding home made cricket bats as they lounge against the wall in front of the old Sea Lane cottages. In 1931 the occupants of the five dwellings were the Dales, and the families Lewis, Hughes, Pescott and Norris. Jefferies Lane is to the left of the last of the houses visible here. All had gone by 1936 (see Plate 92).

Plate 135. The same view in 1993 with Sea Lane seen as a well established dual carriageway to the seaside. The central avenue of Ilex trees survives but there is no trace of the cottages. It is doubtful whether the low flint wall is part of the original. Jefferies Lane can be seen behind the dog walker.

Plate 136. With rounded metal windows and rendered walls the new Sea Lane houses had an almost art deco appearance. The finish is attractive when well maintained but at a greater cost than for brick examples. The final development of Goring Hall Estate did not occur until the early 1960s.

Plate 137. Few Goring residents knew that there was once a railway line down Sea Lane! It was not however a branch from the Southern Railway but a contractors line for the conveyance of materials when the concrete roads were being laid. Tippler wagons can be seen on the track in this 1937 view. The cost of widening was a mere £13,000. The Court House can be seen in the background. The age of the old Court House cannot be ascertained because the deeds were lost in the last century.

Plate 138. Nutley Drive and associated roads were established just after the Second World War. Gradually the entire area from Sea Place to Sea Lane 'filled in' as nursery land was sold for the building of homes. On the whole the homes were of a superior style resulting in Goring becoming the 'right end' of Worthing town.

Plate 139. This pre-development illustration shows Sea Lane on 5 January 1934. In the Winter months the road was impassable. Again the primary features are the enormous boundary walls of the Goring Hall Estate on the left and Jefferies Lane on the right. Nearer to the sea is Beach House and an adjacent pumping house which pumps the water of an underground stream to the sea.

Plate 140. This is one occasion where the 1993 view is more attractive than the early scene. With the 55 year old concrete road still in good shape, the Ilex trees framing the view and with a rich variety of domestic architecture it is clear that there are far worse places to live! The drain in the foreground is a reminder of the extensive drainage work which was necessary prior to large scale development.

Malthouse Cottages

Plate 141. At the end of the attractive Jefferies Lane, which retains much of its 'old world charm', are Malthouse Cottages. Dating from the early 19th century much of the building was indeed originally a malthouse. In 1880 the building was sold for £600 and converted into cottages. This provided accommodation for seven families with two more units being added to the terrace at the turn of the century. Apparently Jefferies Lane was once called 'The Bottom of the Sack', but this may have been a colloquialism or a corruption of 'Cul de Sac'.

Plate 142. If anything the cottages look to be in better shape in this 1993 view compared with the 1932 picture above. They are certainly a welcome survivor from the past. A small twitten leads from the end of Jefferies Lane to the Goring Road. Mabel Baker who has lived in Goring for over 80 years lives in the terrace and her sister Gertrude Lish and niece Mary live in Courtlands Terrace.

Plate 143. The lane takes its name from the naturalist and poet Richard Jefferies. Born in 1848 his stay in Goring was a short one. After moving to the south coast for health reasons he finally moved from Worthing to Goring in 1886. Initially staying at the Peacock Hotel with his wife and two children he finally moved into a house called 'Sea View'.

Plate 144. 'Sea View' in 1908 when it was possible to literally have a view of the sea across the undeveloped marshland. The building still stands in Jefferies Lane and the above plaque was appended to the property in 1939. Jefferies was confined to the property in his last days and at the age of 39 he died from tuberculosis in an upstairs room on 14 August 1887. The property changed hands for £3000 in 1955. There are a number of other old properties in the lane.

The Beach

Plate 145. For many years the area between the Goring Road and the sea was an undrained marshland which was very susceptible to flooding. However in the 1930s comprehensive changes took place with roads, drains and sewers being laid. Despite the absence of the present greensward there were still plenty of visitors in summer and as can be seen in this 1928 picture at the end of Sea Lane a miscellany of temporary buildings and caravans had sprung up.

Plate 146. It was perhaps ironic that in 1993 it was a very different form of caravan which arrived on the greensward on the Goring/Ferring border. The unwelcome travellers may have been tinkers or gipsies or simply mobile tarmac merchants. They had to be removed by due process of law. These parasites contribute absolutely nothing to society in terms of rates or taxes and they leave litter and mess wherever they choose to invade. There is obviously one elderly resident who is determined to carry on as usual!

Plate 147. The four cars visible here suggest a date in the late 1920s. They are parked at the bottom of Sea Lane next to the site of the present Sea Lane Cafe. The six foot flint wall on the right was the boundary of the Goring Hall Estate. A few flints can still be found in the hedgerow. In the distance a couple take the ozone.

Plate 148. There are no cars whatsoever in this 1993 photograph at the same location. That is because a sizeable car park for today's army of motorists has been constructed a few yards to the east of Sea Lane. The Goring sea front has increased in popularity in recent years due to greater public mobility and the formidable growth in water sports. A handful of fishermen still keep their boats between Sea Place and Sea Lane, Ferring.

Plate 149. The Brighton Boy Scouts football team visited Goring in August 1911. Writing from "Tent 16 Goring Camp" Fred wrote to his Dad in Hove "We played the Boys Brigade, about twice as big as us and licked us 6–3. Love to Mum." Sadly there is no indication of which of the eleven players is Fred.

Plate 150. This 1933 postcard shows the remarkable scale of the Goring Hall Estate boundary wall which ran almost the entire distance between Sea Lane, Goring and Sea Lane, Ferring. Over the years it must have suffered considerable damage from heavy seas. There seems to be an outfall visible and this suggests a location near to the Plantation.

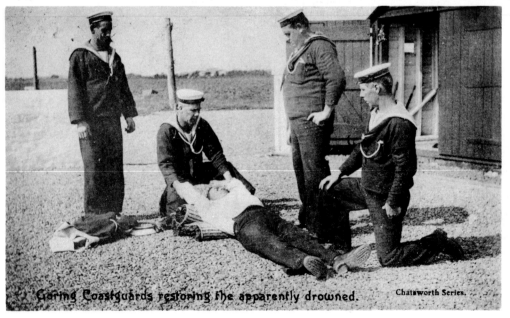

Goring Coastguards restoring the apparently drowned.

Chatsworth Series.

Plate 151. In the early days of the 19th century three coastguard cottages were built at the end of the Plantation, across the greensward from Aldsworth Avenue. There were still smuggling activities at that time, a position which continued until about 1830. In 1749 three smugglers received death sentences as a result of a Goring smuggling affray during which a dragoon was killed. Mr Goldfinch was the Coastguard at the turn of the century and Mr Roper operated the lifeboat. The cottages fell into disrepair shortly after 1900. This very old card was postally used in 1906 and the caption reads "Goring Coastguards restoring the apparently drowned".

1987 Hurricane

Plate 152. On 16 October 1987 a Hurricane hit the Goring area causing widespread devastation. Trees were uprooted, walls and fences were felled, tiles and even whole roofs were torn off and property was severely damaged. The heavy seas dragged the shingle on the beach back by many yards and for the first time in decades the remains of the walls and foundations of the old Coastguard Cottages at the end of the Plantation were exposed (see bricks middle foreground).

Plate 153. At the height of the Hurricane, thankfully in the small hours, beach huts were hurled into the air and the seafront houses along Marine Crescent faced the full force of the wind. Garage doors flew off and even street lights were buckled. Looking like a battlefield this was the "morning after" scene just east of Sea Lane Cafe.

THE CRESCENT, GORING ROAD, GORING-BY-SEA   3760

Plate 154. Produced just post Second World War this postcard is captioned "The Crescent, Goring Road". It shows the shopping area around Mulberry Parade. Caffyns is still very much in business at the same premises on the right, although Worthing Dairies next door have long gone. The building with the 'Power Ethyl' advertisement on the side was formerly Chase Cottage which later became a branch the National Provincial Bank. (see also Plate 156).

Plate 155. In this 1993 view the buildings to both the left and right are the same as Plate 154 but the small parade in the middle around the Locost supermarket area is new. There is as usual more traffic in the later scene. The old keep left bollards are more stylish than their replacements. The security store is unfortunately a sign of the times and the growing crime rate.

Goring by Sea. Sussex.

Plate 156. This spectacular postcard by the Worthing Portrait Company was sent from Goring to Littlehampton in December 1911. The cottage on the right is Chase Cottage which was occupied by Mary Chase in the mid-19th century and later by Mr Hayler, Clerk to the Goring Parish Council. In later years thatch gave way to tiles on the roof. It was located on what is now the slip road in front of the Locost Supermarket. The National Provincial Bank had an agency there before it became a branch in its own right. The same old story prevailed; it was demolished in 1960. Note Courtlands Terrace (and the watermill) in the background.

Plate 157. Virtually the same view in 1993 with cars and commercial activity in abundance. Courtlands Terrace is common to both photographs but the Goring Road was widened and straightened at this point in 1934. The pedestrian crossing is a lifeline for pedestrians and a source of delay for motorists!

Plate 158. This is the only known photograph of another of Goring's classic cottages. This thatched cottage was occupied by the Misses Olliver when they moved from Courtlands in 1899, at the time that Mr Schweder took over the lease. There was normally a goat in the garden and their many cats were often seen looking out of the window. This time the planners could not be blamed as the cottages burned to the ground in 1916. The end wall of Courtlands Terrace is visible on the left which dates the photograph as 1910–1915.

Plate 159. The Ollivers' cottage was replaced by the shops and flats shown here. Denyer News, formerly Courtlands Newsagents, Moseley the Jewellers and Mulberry Meats (formerly Woods') are well established Goring businesses. The common feature in this 1993 view is of course the end wall of Courtlands Terrace.

Plate 160. A wider view of the south side of the Goring Road in 1987 shows the two distinct styles of the Courtlands Terrace buildings. The later shops on the north side of the road were constructed in 1959.

Plate 161. The tiny sapling on the left has now grown into the tree featured in the picture above. Here the north side of the Goring Road has yet to be built upon and judging by the telegraph poles GPO communications were all above ground. There were no satellites or dishes in the early 1950s! A green double deck Southdown bus approaches and all the cars visible are pre-war – and made in England.

Plate 162. In 1931 a total of seventeen names were shown in the street directory for Courtlands Terrace. They included the Goring station porter Charlie Challen and a sub-office of the Worthing Gas, Light and Coke Company. There has always been a couple of shops at the end of the terrace, in this case the store of F. Hazelgrove selling, amongst other things, Rowntree's Cocoa. It is now a Funeral Director's office.

Plate 163. One of Goring's jolly shopkeepers was the late Ethel Cornford, Godmother of the author's wife Carol. Old fashioned 'over the counter' service was provided. When photographed in 1969 she ran the end store in Courtlands Terrace. Her family ran the Bull Inn in 1931 and from the same address ran another business, W Cornford & Son, Builders. In addition to a full range of groceries she also sold Milk of Magnesia. There was no time for subtlety in those days! The 'shop' is now a Doctor's surgery.

Plate 164. Just west of Tudor Cottage once stood Beale's Garage, later Goring-by-Sea Garage and eventually Searle's Garage. In this 1934 view the middle of the three names applied. Cleveland petrol was 1/3 (about 6p) per gallon. The sign shows that a car could be hired for £1 per day – then about half a weeks pay. There was an old gravel pit on the north side of the Goring Road at this location and two old thatched cottages called Whitehall Cottages. When Searle's Garage was opened the famous racing driver Stirling Moss performed the ceremony. He landed by helicopter in West Park.

Plate 165. Today houses have sprung-up along the Goring Road, the old garage has been demolished and replaced by Homesearle House. Street lighting has been provided. The Tudor Cottage and the grass verge have survived.

Plate 166. Almost certainly Goring's oldest building is Ye Olde Tudor Cottage. There is no doubt that the cottage dates back to the middle ages. The windows upstairs are at floor level and almost inevitably stories about connections with smuggling have survived over the years. As can be seen in about 1915 a small sweet shop which also offered teas was attached to the building. It was in danger of demolition in 1937 but it was thankfully saved from the grasp of the road wideners.

Plate 167. Mr Cozzi ran a hardware store in the mid-1950s on the last piece of undeveloped ground on the south side of the Goring Road. This pose was typical as he always had time for a chat over his 'garden' wall. There would not be much of a market for his coal bunkers today! He sold everything from Pink paraffin to wrought iron gates.

Plate 168. Ye Olde Tudor Cottage as just plain No 201 Goring Road, in 1986. The thatched roof had been replaced by tiles about a decade earlier. The side door has been converted to a window and additional windows have been added. The property has been extended at the rear. The building on the left was Millns cycle shop in the 1950s and 1960s. Courtlands Terrace can be seen in the background.

Plate 169. This building was known as Southdown House, although for many years it was a guest house called Holiday House. As Holiday House it is seen in 1915; a date confirmed by the Post Office cancellation on the reverse of the postcard. Another card shows the building was called 'The Wurlie'. It was demolished in April 1974 to make way for a new block of flats which also carries the name of Southdown House.

Plate 170. Despite the high volume of today's traffic there are fewer people killed on the roads now than there were 55 years ago. One thing is for sure; there is nothing new about road accidents in Goring. The author photographed this incident on the corner of Marlborough Road and Clive Avenue in 1958. A Standard Vanguard had overturned resulting in much local excitement.

Plate 171. Many parents have been grateful over the past four decades for the education afforded to their children at West Park School. The growth in population in the 1940s and 1950s resulted in Elm Grove and Goring School becoming overwhelmed. West Park opened in September 1952 with the subsequent addition of outbuildings and a partially handicapped unit. The school is situated in Marlborough Road.

1741 Goring Lane Near Worthing

Plate 172. Lady Stern described the Goring Road in the 1920s as a narrow, dark, muddy lane overhung by trees. If two cars met one would have to stop and pull over. This pre-1908 scene shows some locals walking down the lane towards West Worthing. The road was then known as Goring Lane. It would be a further quarter of a century before improvements arrived.

Plate 173. This unusual shot shows the village thatcher at work. His ladder is against the chimney of Ivy Cottage, beyond Chase Cottage at the western end of Goring Lane. With a thatcher's mate holding the ladder children gaze at the novel sight of a camera.

Plate 174. Looking east the thatched roof just visible behind the rustic horse and cart is that of Southfield Place Barn belonging to Three Furlong Farm. This is now the junction of Shaftesbury Avenue and the Goring Road! The card was posted in July 1914.

Goring Lane, Goring-by-Sea.   Dunn

Plate 175. Arthur Dunn was a well known local photographer who lived at Walton House in Sea Place in the early 1930s. He took this photograph of a couple in Goring Lane immediately opposite the junction with Sea Place. The houses just visible on the right mostly survive as does Sea Place Garage, which can just be seen with 'BP' oil containers. The date is about 1932.

Courtlands

Plate 176. This is the original Courtlands built by the banker William Olliver (1794–1854) in about 1820. He was the owner of extensive tracts of land in Goring. The house was built near the site of the ancient Brook Barn settlement. The original house was of modest size, these young ladies are posing on the north balcony in 1902.

Garden Fete, Courtlands July 1st 1914.
Goring VY Sec.

Plate 177. The building was purchased by Mr Paul Schweder in 1902. This wealthy gentleman purchased land all around the house so that by 1907 he owned land from Sea Place to Alinora Avenue and from the south side of Courtlands Lake to the railway line. He significantly enlarged the building and imported many fine fixtures and fittings from other country houses at home and abroad. He enlarged the gardens and outbuildings using local bricks produced from the brickworks he owned just south of the railway line. Here a garden fete is being held in the grounds, on 1 July 1914.

Plate 178. Lady Somerset once gave Schweder some cuttings for the Courtlands Gardens and there was an avenue of lime trees down the line of Parklands Avenue. Schweder built estate walls and a north lodge, just south of Goring Lane (Road). The lodge, seen here, was demolished in 1963 to make way for the inner service road. Schweder died in 1936 aged 79 and all his furniture and effects were sold on 15 November 1937, by which time housing had reached the eastern side of the estate. Schweder was well known for his various disputes with local authorities and utility companies.

Plate 179. From 1941 to 1945 Courtlands was taken over by the military and in 1945 it was designated as a post operative hospital with 52 beds. The title given to it in the 1950s was Courtlands Convalescent Hospital. Conversion cost a total of £31,332. The hospital was formally opened by Her Royal Highness Princess Elizabeth on 19 May 1951. Here the future Queen meets the medical staff and employees. I wonder if she remembers her visit to Goring?

Plate 180. Although somewhat run down during the war years the grand surroundings provided by Paul Schweder were still in evidence for recovering patients to enjoy. From time to time the grounds have been used for craft fairs and fetes. The last patient left Courtlands about 1972 and since then it has been used by the Local Health Authority. There has been concern recently about the deteriorating building fabric and neglected gardens.

Plate 181. In the days when Worthing Borough Council could afford to regularly cut grass verges and pick up the grass afterwards most public places were well looked after. The beautiful Courtlands Lake, seen here in 1986, was well maintained and the gardens were a sheer joy for all who were privileged to see them. Now even the debris from the 1987 hurricane has not been completely cleared. At least this is another of Goring's fine country houses which is still standing.

Sea Place

SEA PLACE, GORING, JAN 5 34

Plate 182. As Worthing at first slowly and then quickly grew it spread west from Grand Avenue and on to Wallace and George V Avenues. By the early 1930s Sea Place was sharply in focus. The few residents enjoyed their first dust-cart rubbish collection on 2 April 1929. On 5 January 1934 the road had still not been adopted and mud and puddles were the order of the day.

Plate 183. This was the same scene in 1993 between Harvey Road and Courtlands Close looking north towards the Goring Road. Sea Place Manor has a history dating back to 1321. In 1512 Sea Place Farm was acquired by Robert Sherburn, Bishop of Chichester, and given by him to the Dean and Chapter. The only original building which formed part of the old Sea Place Manor is located between Smugglers Walk and Moat Way.

Plate 184. It is hard to remember a tranquil Goring Road but when photographed by the redoubtable Mr Dunn in 1934 it had been widened but was not built-up. The view from east to west shows Sea Place Garage on the left with Southfield Place Barn (Shaftesbury Avenue) on the right. A Southdown bus overtakes a van on the new 'fast' highway.

Plate 185. Now this is more like it! The house on the far left remains and the traffic coming away from the Shaftesbury Avenue traffic lights will be familiar to most residents. Crossing the road is nigh impossible unless ones running is up to olympic standards! From 6p in 1934 petrol had risen to 230p per gallon in 1993. Sadly the giant elm trees have all gone leaving a rather barren scene. The Shaftesbury Avenue road junction was rebuilt in 1968.

SEA PLACE. GORING-BY-SEA.   Dunn.

Plate 186. The south end of Sea Place in the 1930s with a couple of 'flappers' posing in the sunshine opposite Farm View. Sea Place developed in piecemeal fashion with a rich variety of architecture. Baker's, Kidd's and Chesham nurseries were all sold for housing; the prospect of rising land values being too tempting for some. Eventually Sea Place became a metalled road.

SEA PLACE, WORTHING.   6510

Plate 187. This building still stands at Sea Place serving the yachting fraternity and other visitors. In the 1930s it sported a sign which read, "Cafe, morning coffee, beach trays, tea and minerals." The old flint wall which runs in front of the building delineates the eastern boundary of the medieval Sea Place Manor.

THE BEACH, GORING-BY-SEA.   Dunn.

Plate 188. A Goring Beach scene from 1934 near to the present site of Worthing Yacht Club. The mainly shingle beach with a few sandy patches still attracts visitors but with local seaweed problems and the attraction of virtually guaranteed sunshine at foreign destinations the old fashioned British seaside holiday has been in decline for many years. Having said that it is still hard to get a parking place along the greensward on a fine summers day! Worthing Corporation sensibly purchased a 50 acre strip of land between Sea Place and Sea Lane, Ferring as a public recreation area for £33,250.

Plate 189. Smugglers Farm, Sea Place, in 1935 before all the land was sold-off for housing. Another postcard in the series shows cattle grazing on Smugglers Farm. The message written in 1933 states "This farm is just opposite our bungalow. A nice homely sight."

Plate 190. The attractive northern entrance to Rose Walk. Rose Walk is near to the eastern extremity of the present Goring Parish boundary. This was another residential road which grew rapidly in the late 1920s and early 1930s.

THE ROSE WALK, GORING-BY-SEA.

Plate 191. George V Avenue looking south across the roundabout at the junction with the Goring Road. The George Hotel then dispensed ales from the Kemp Town Brewery at Brighton but now purveys the products of Bass/Charrington. In 1950 there were no double yellow lines and few parking restrictions. Only short sighted motorists would miss the stylish Keep Left signs.

GEORGE V AVENUE, WEST WORTHING.

Plate 192. 55 years separates these impressions of the Goring Road from the George V Avenue roundabout. The George Hotel pub sign has become simply 'The George', the telephone box has changed but is in the same location, the telegraph poles are in about the same place and the buildings on the right are common to both pictures. However on this 1993 morning the traffic was simply horrendous. The traffic island has become a haven for pedestrians while they wait for somebody to give way.

Plate 193. There are three cars on the Goring Road in this pre-war view and twenty-one in the modern view. The street lights are modest by comparison but what is perhaps surprising is that just beyond the large elm tree the road became derestricted with no speed limit, not that the Austin 7 approaching could achieve a speed much in excess of 40 mph!

Plate 194. Strictly this shows the Goring Road in West Worthing looking east from the George V Avenue roundabout. This extremely busy shopping centre is often congested as car-bound shoppers try to park within a few yards of the store they are visiting. A single pelican pedestrian crossing replaced a zebra crossing at each end of the parade a few years ago.

Plate 195. In 1950 there were still a few private houses on the south side of the Goring Road and there was no inner service road. There were grass verges on the north side and on the far left is the Post Office which subsequently moved 'around the corner' into George V Avenue. Note the handful of automobiles.

GORING ROAD, WORTHING. 5806

Plate 196. High Summer in August 1948 with hardly a building between Durrington-on-Sea station and Highdown Hill. British Railways had just been formed as a result of Nationalisation, a fact broadcast by the lettering on the locomotive's tender. K Class 2-6-0 No 32344 heads east on a mixed freight from the Portsmouth direction. There is not a trace of Maybridge Estate. In 1929 Sir Alan Cobham made public flights from the Field Place airfield to 'promote air mindedness'. His air liner was called 'Youth of Britain'.

Plate 197. Between 1949 and 1960 Maybridge Estate slowly but steadily took shape. The eastern end of The Strand and the Quadrant were built first. This shows the progress by 1952 taken from the south west. In the left foreground is Ardingly Drive and Limbrick Crossing. There are no houses whatsoever on Palatine Road and Goring Green Estate was not even a twinkle in the planners eye.

Plate 198. The Strand Parade circa 1954. One Austin 7 Ruby saloon car and a few bicycles are the only vehicular traffic. The vacant lot on the left was later filled by the construction of the Golden Lion pub. A temporary Golden Lion was opened near Durrington station in 1950. The shops on the south side, Lloyds Bank building and the Sixth Form College were all later additions.

STRAND PARADE, GORING BY SEA, SUSSEX.

Plate 199. As already seen so many times in 'Goring and Ferring Past and Present' comparisons over the years can be dramatic. This plate should be compared with Plate 196. Other than for the sanctuary of Highdown Hill in the distance the whole area has been developed. Durrington-on-Sea station was opened and Durrington Bridge built in July 1937 in anticipation of the new estates. On 6 June 1987 Class 33/2 diesel No. 33212 heads the 05.50 from Exeter St Davids towards Brighton.

Plate 200. The Royal Air Force Fighter Command made use of the Inland Revenue site to the south of Durrington station during the 1939/45 war. A military hospital was built towards the end of the war to enable returning soldiers to convalesce. It was occupied by the Inland Revenue from 1949 and now some 1500 employees work at the complex. The old South Block seen here survives but a new block was being built in 1993 on the foreground field, more recently a staff car park. Behind the site to the west is the old Goring gas holder.

Flower show and Sports at Field Place. Jy 25th 1912 - The May Pole -

Plate 201. There has been a manor house at Field Place since the 14th century. For over 300 years the manor was in the hands of the Cooke family. In the 18th century while in the hands of the Henty family the house was extensively altered and the present frontage dates from about 1800. This rare postcard shows village girls dancing around the Maypole at the Coronation celebrations in July 1912.

Plate 202. Field Place is now owned by Worthing Borough Council and the site is used as a sports and social centre, especially for lawn and indoor bowling. The manor still contains the Oak Room which boasts some fine Jacobean panelling. There are some fine flint buildings in the grounds. This shows the house in December 1986. Field Place and Maybridge Estate are now outside of the Parish of Goring.

FERRING

As Highdown Hill is largely contained within the Parish of Ferring it is probable that Ferring is even older than Goring. The Hill has had an important strategic position over the centuries and although only 269 feet high it enjoys an unrivalled view across the Coastal Plain.

As with Goring, the Parish of Ferring has been owned by a succession of aristocratic families with considerable influence. However again it is the Domesday Book which provides a useful indicator in recognising Ferring or Feringes (Ferringes according to Horsfield – 1835) as a place in the possessions of the Bishop of Chichester. Later prominent family names include the Westbrookes, the Richardsons and the Hentys. The Manor House was founded at a very early date and was the occasional home of the Bishops of Chichester.

The largely agricultural community was remarkably stable in terms of numbers. Between the date of the Norman Conquest and the start of the 20th century, a period of over 800 years, there were between 30 and 50 households in the whole of Ferring. The population in 1801 was 238, in 1851 inhabitants totalled 312 and by 1901 it was back to 243. The population of 256 in 1921 then leapt to 795 in 1931 as the developers moved in. By 1971 the census showed 4292 people resident in the Parish, which is near saturation point for the land available.

Ferring has resisted repeated attempts for it to join the Borough of Worthing. The vital Goring Gap has effectively created a natural break, or border, with its Goring neighbour. In fact at one of the many popular votes on the subject only a single resident voted for a union with Worthing. Ferring is not entirely without pavements or street lighting but most of the streets, drives and avenues have none. In the past this resulted in Ferring residents enjoying reduced domestic rates because they could legitimately claim to be making fewer demands on the provision of services. However with the introduction of Poll Tax and then Council Tax the advantages have not been so obvious. However these earlier decisions have resulted in Ferring having an atmosphere of its own as walkers are obliged to stroll down the roads of Ferring.

The Village of Ferring has also managed to retain its identity by virtue of its topography and its geographical position. There is the already mentioned Goring Gap with only the coastal road and Goring Way as links from the east. The northern boundary in terms of buildings (but not land) is the Littlehampton Road which forms a clearly delineated 'break' with only Franklands and Langbury Lane forming direct routes to the village. Due to the River Rife and Kingston Gorse there is no western road access at all, except for the Littlehampton Road. All of this has resulted in Ferring being something of an 'island'.

Ferring has been very fortunate indeed in being able to prevent the demolition of many of its old cottages. There is a rich choice of dwelling dating back to the 17th and 18th centuries and other buildings which have even earlier origins. Part of one of the original manor houses still stands and the whole of the other is extant. The interesting Parish Church is a particular focal point. Many of the old farms have disappeared over time and perhaps Ferring has not done quite as well as Goring in preserving old flint barns but there are still some fine examples to be seen.

The residential development of Ferring has seen the construction of a truly mixed bag of houses and bungalows. Unlike many of Goring's streets, attractive as many of them are, Ferring's roads are shorter, narrower and less concentric. There is a good selection of mainly small 'local' stores. There are but a few industrial premises and most employment is outside of the Parish. There are only two public houses, which also double as restaurants. Ferring boasts a small library, a Primary School, Youth Centre and other facilities. There has never been a Ferring railway station but the village is served by buses.

The village has a community spirit and there are a number of well established organisations, such as the Residents Association, the Parish Council, Rifers Youth Club, Ferring Retirement Club and many others. They all contribute in one way and another to the preservation of Ferring. More recently a Ferring Charter has been proposed to try and persuade residents to adopt a responsible approach to the village environment.

It is interesting to note that in all of the older maps of Ferring the natural division of the village is between east and west Ferring but with the coming of the railway and the position of shopping developments it is now more common to hear of a north and south Ferring 'divide'. Fortunately the identity of Ferring has not been diluted by these labels.

As with the Goring area Ferring is still regularly under attack from all sides and occasionally from within in terms of unwelcome developments. One only has to review the Parish Council minutes to see just how many unacceptable proposals for change are turned down. Some want to extend buildings in an inappropriate style, some would rather fell a preserved tree than pay for its proper maintenance, some would try to build three bungalows where there is only reasonable space for two. But the main problem is those who would attack the few open spaces, such as a recent proposal to build on the Goring Gap. Of course there needs to be change and innovation to meet changing times but not at the expense of what is left and worth preserving.

The relative isolation of Ferring has helped retain its identity but it has meant that for many a motor car has become a necessity and this has reflected even in Ferring traffic volumes. There are few parking places available outside of Ferring Post Office on a Saturday morning! The Ferring level crossing gates are a major source of delay. The old centre of the village was helped by the construction of Greystoke Road and more recently some cobbles and bollards have been added to retain its rural character.

There are over 100 photographs of Ferring in this book; almost exactly one third of the total. I have tried to show the many transitions which have occurred over the past century. While some changes have been significant others have been very subtle indeed. As stated elsewhere the intervening decades have not been forgotten and indeed in terms of South Ferring there was very little to photograph before the late 1920s. While not purporting to be a history of Ferring I have tried to cram a large number of facts and figures into the captions.

The journey starts to the north of the Parish, crosses the railway line and after passing through the heart of the old village continues to the sea. From south Ferring the coverage crosses to Sea Lane on the eastern boundary before returning north via East Ferring House.

While living in Goring it seems as though most walks with the family Spaniel either end up along the Rife, on Highdown or along the western end of Goring Hall Drive and past the derelict Manor Farm; all being in the Parish of Ferring. To my knowledge this is the first pictorial appreciation of the village of Ferring and I hope it will find favour.

Ferring 1913

Lower Ecclesden Farm

Ham Spinney

New Mill Cottage

Ecclesden Manor

Old Chalk Pit

Old Chalk Pit

Old Chalk Pit

Highdown Copse

Rough Piece

Miller's Cottage

Highdown Hill

Old Chalk Pit

Old Chalk Pit

The Miller's Tomb

Old Chalk Pit

Chalk Pit

Old Chalk Pit

Old Chalk Pits

Hill Barn

Hangleton Lane

Hangleton

Florence Villa

North Barn

Hangleton Farm

Hogtrough

New Barn

Hangleton Farm

Pledge's Cottage

Franklands Green

New Barn Cottages

FERRING

New Inn

Acres 1052·898

School

Vicarage

West Ferring

East Ferring Farm

St. Andrew's Church

Rose Cottage

Park Barn

The Grange (Manor House)

East Ferring House

Manor Farm

East Ferring

Kingston House

Kingston

KINGSTON

Acres 554·335

Plate 203. From the top of Highdown Hill the whole of the Ferring Parish can be seen. An outline history of the hill appears in the Goring section. Although postally used in 1947 this postcard view of sheep grazing on the hill was probably recorded in the late 1930s. The flint wall once ran from the upper part of Highdown to the sea, effectively dividing Goring and Ferring. A small underground reservoir was built here in the 1960s.

Plate 204. While Goring has lost most of its old cottages Ferring is peppered with numerous old buildings which greatly contribute to the charm of the Parish. Towards the north of the Parish, just south of the Littlehampton Road in Ferring Lane, is the Franklands complex with typical flint walls edged in brick; a magnificent survivor of the Georgian period. The dwellings are now called Jasmine Cottage, Clematis Cottage, Frankland Mews and Franklands Manor.

Plate 205. This view of the then quiet North Ferring Corner was posted from Worthing to Lingfield, Surrey in 1966. The road then formed a 'T' junction with the single lane Littlehampton Road. The junction has since been modified and many of the trees have gone.'

Plate 206. This is the most recent photograph in this book and it shows a view of North Ferring from a helicopter at an elevation of 1000 feet, on 1 August 1993. The former Imperial Tea Lounge, now the Thai Garden Restaurant is bottom right, the curving Langbury Lane is in the centre, Onslow Caravan Park and the Rife are top right, the War Memorial is top left with the Littlehampton Road forming the base of the photograph.

Langbury Lane

Plate 207. The core of the old Ferring village was located entirely within a few hundred yards of St Andrew's Church with only a sprinkling of farm buildings and cottages elsewhere. There was hardly a building north of the railway line but this late 17th century cottage which formed part of Hangleton Farm was one of the few exceptions. This view is dated 1954.

Plate 208. The cottage is located towards the north end of Langbury Lane opposite South Hangleton and it can easily be recognised in the 1993 photograph. The development of North Ferring occurred some years later than South Ferring, although it is interesting to note that in past centuries the only division was between East and West Ferring.

Plate 209. When the railway was opened from Worthing to Lyminster in March 1846 Ferring was not blessed with a station; the nearest being Goring and Angmering. A fine example of a period crossing keepers cottage was provided. Over the years efforts have regularly been made to erect a 'halt' at Ferring but pleas have fallen on deaf ears. The diminutive signalbox was in the national news shortly before demolition in 1988 because 'Fred' the rat bit the crossing signalman! On 5 November 1983 Class 33/2 diesel No. 33204 passes Ferring with the 09.20 Brighton to Exeter train.

Plate 210. A few hundred yards north of Ferring Crossing is Franklands Corner. Old maps show that on the eastern side of the road was Pledge's Cottage, located behind the flint wall on the left. Also behind the wall is the 1727-built Elford House with its 1907 wing extension. This postcard was posted in 1934.

Plate 211. Messrs Claridge Diss & Co have long disappeared from the estate agent scene and their diminutive office at the railway crossing end of Langbury Lane has been swept away. The lane from the New Inn (Henty Arms) to the guide post on the Littlehampton Road was one of the earliest routes out of the village. It now features in a dispute following broken promises to villagers that a roundabout would be provided at the junction of Langbury Lane and the A259.

Plate 212. Without a railway station Ferring villagers have had to rely on omnibuses for local journeys; or walk over a mile to Goring station. Bus services commenced in Edwardian times but even photographs from the 1950s, such as this view of one of Southdown's few Dennis buses heading for Ferring on a service '31F', look dated.

Plate 213. The Henty Arms was so named in 1936 after the best known family in the village. Since its 1830 construction date it had been known as the New Inn. For many years it served ale from the Henty and Constable Brewery but the now closed brewery was taken over by Watneys in 1955 and the pub disposed of to Friary Meux. The public house has unfortunately had its flint walls painted over; an act which would not be appreciated by either Sir John Betjeman or Alec Clifton-Taylor! Nevertheless the building has a firm place in the history of Ferring.

Plate 214. Onslow Parade is the nearest shopping centre to the residents of Ferring who live north of the railway line, although the 'sell everything' garden centres on the Littlehampton Road may have affected business in recent years. The terrace includes a Doctor's surgery, a pharmacy and a 'chippy'. In the right background is Ferring Village Hall which in 1993 is still well used.

Plate 215. This photograph was taken 45 years earlier than the above and there have been surprisingly few changes. The grass verge in front of the service road has been paved, the telegraph post has disappeared and the traffic has increased.

Plate 216. There are often queues of cars outside the shops in Onslow Parade not shopping but waiting for the railway barriers to clear. There have been complaints of long delays allegedly due to the signals and barriers being controlled remotely from Lancing. What would seem a more likely reason is that three times per hour trains are booked to cross each other which means motorists waiting for more than one train.

Plate 217. In this view from the 1950s the new block backing onto the crossing keeper's cottage had not been built and old Lilac Cottage was located on the opposite side of the road from Onslow Parade. Crossing warning signs are located in a similar position in both pictures. The black Morris 8 car would however be illegally parked if 1993 regulations applied.

Plate 218. This very old postcard was sent to Brighton in August 1906. Part of the message reads 'I am staying here, don't you think its pretty'. The quaint Rose Cottage remains and the side window still looks out onto the pavement. The chimney brickwork detectable on the east face, the red window dressings and quoins are equally obvious today. If the little girl is still alive she will now be in her nineties. This is Ferring Street looking north.

Plate 219. The survival of such buildings as Rose Cottage makes Ferring special and most of the owners take great pride in maintaining their properties to a high standard. Another survivor can be glimpsed behind Rose Cottage; Landalls, an 18th century cottage which was once two cottages and Vine Cottage which many years ago was used as the village school. A deep well at the rear of the properties has been filled in.

Plate 220. Despite the 60 years between these photographs the trees in the centre of the scene look almost identical. The last of the modern shops on the right is Ferring Post Office and behind it the end window of Ferring Village Hall can be seen. Lilac Cottage which stood opposite Onslow Parade has been demolished and replaced by Pump Court. Recorded in February 1993.

Plate 221. In 1933 the Village Hall served a similar purpose as it does today. However the population then was 800 whereas today it is at saturation point at 4300. As usual a bit of old flint wall still exists on the right and the luxury of pavements now grace both sides of the street. The Hall was built in 1924 and extended in 1929.

Ferring Lane.

Plate 222. This postcard view will bring back memories for any villager who can remember the year 1932. Even in those days there was a garage for motor cars on the corner of Ferring Street and Sea Lane. Next to the garage was a dairy and other small shops. The War Memorial stands as a silent sentinel over the scene.

Plate 223. Virtually the entire corner has now been taken over by John Cooper Garages dealing in a mixture of British and Japanese cars. Coopers won the motor racing World Constructors Championship in both 1959 and 1960. The two houses beyond the garage still serve a useful purpose as a small supermarket and the pylons installed in 1932/33 are obtrusive but vital to Ferring's power supplies.

FERRING-ON-SEA VILLAGE

Plate 224. This view is pre-war but not as early as the 1932 postcard (Plate 222). The dairy now carries the name Fuente & Scarce Ltd and the same name appears on the van outside. The terrace also includes a newsagent and a draper. According to signs the dairy sells both pure milk and Bovril! One of the two trees can be seen today, albeit in a perpetually pruned state. To the right, on the opposite side of the road stood the now demolished Daisy Cottage.

Plate 225. Just south of the War Memorial can be found the oldest part of the village. Ferring Street and Church Lane both contain some architectural gems. At the junction of Ferring Street and Rife Way was Ferring's first school. Opened in 1873 with some 25 children attending, it was in continuous use until 1952. Just south of this site is the 1965-built library (cost £11,500) which was described at the time as 'a monstrosity' but apparently functional. Further down the west side of Ferring Street is the unique Yew Tree Cottage, seen here. It changed hands in 1932 for £425! The single storey building with flint walls and thatched roof originally comprised four rooms built around a central chimney stack. It is over 200 years old.

20921. SUSSEX COTTAGE. FERRING-BY-SEA.

FERRING.

191824

Plate 227. It is amazing to relate that in 1993 the dip in the flint wall seen just in front of the children above (and Yew Tree Cottage) is unchanged, despite the 85 year time span. Pavements have been provided and more recently an attractive traffic calming scheme using bollards and flint cobbles was built. On the right only one of two cottages survive on what was originally a dairy farm owned by the Hentys. Nearby a commemorative tree was planted by the active Ferring Parish Council in Jubilee year, 1977.

Plate 226. This postcard was posted from Ferring to Stirling in Scotland on New Year's Eve 1908 and shows four children standing in Ferring Street with the camera pointing north. Behind the youngsters are four houses of Georgian and Victorian vintage. These include Barberry Lodge, Glebe Gate, Brierley and the Coach House. All of these once formed part of the old Ferring Vicarage complex.

Plate 228. A little further along Ferring Street just before the corner into Church Lane on the west side are Smugglers Cottage and its petite Annex. Although stories can become exaggerated over time there is ample evidence of smuggling activities in the Ferring area, including a shoot-out in 1720 involving Customs Officers and upwards of 60 armed men. The buildings are seen here on a postcard posted from Goring on 30 July 1927.

Plate 229. A photographic reproduction of a map depicting the heart of Ferring as it was 100 years ago. On the right is the Goring Hall Drive running between East Ferring and Manor Farms. Only Sea Lane connects the two halves of the village. There were only a few cottages north of the School (by the present War Memorial) and the main buildings comprise the Vicarage, the Church and the cottages around, the Greystoke and the Grange. South of Brook Barn and Home Farm, Ferringham Lane ends abruptly with only a footpath south to Tudor Close barn etc.

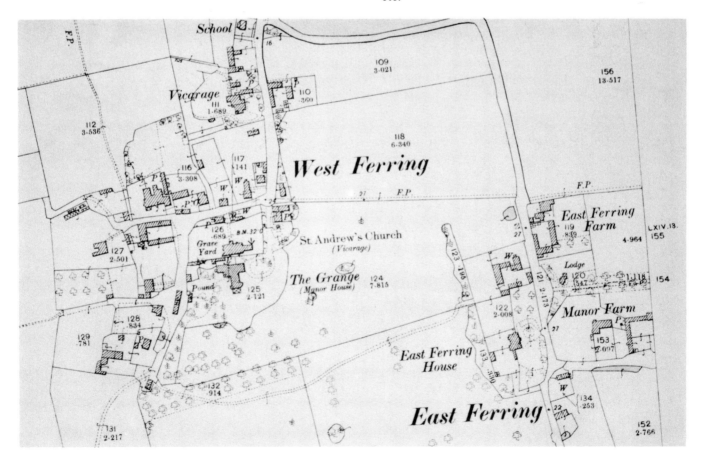

Plate 230. This old cottage is situated almost opposite Smugglers Cottage. Once a two storey thatched building it was seriously damaged by fire in 1930 and rebuilt as a single storey dwelling. Just visible on the right is the wall of Grange Cottage, originally the Lodge and Coach House for Ferring Grange.

Plate 231. As usual with the older buildings many were the home of more than one family, although evidence in this case is not concrete. This 1910 postcard shows the upstairs dormer windows to advantage and the pre-fire thatched roof. The building is now called simply 'The Old Cottage'.

Plate 232. One of the delights of Ferring is being able to take photographs which are decades apart and after comparison conclude that little has changed. This only applies of course to the older 'hub' of the Ferring community around the Church. Taken in 1993 this view shows Smugglers Cottage on the right and Evergreen Cottage on the left. The latter was built in the 17th century and extended in the 18th century.

Plate 233. Over 60 years before the above scene was recorded this card was sent from 'Hillview', Ferring to Havant in Hampshire. The trees and the flint wall look little different to the contemporary view but the display cabinet has given way to a garden shed. A Smugglers Cottage outbuilding was once used as a laundry for Ferring Grange.

Church Lane

Plate 234. Ferring Cricket Ground is slightly off the beaten track a few yards down a footpath called Little Twitten at the eastern end of Church Lane. Like Goring, Ferring has a fine cricketing tradition. The footpath on the left is used by pedestrians and dog walkers as a direct link between Goring Hall Drive and Ferring village. On the right is the cricket ground and a large sightscreen can be seen in the background.

FERRING-ON-SEA, CHURCH LANE.

V5484

Plate 235. A delightful day in 1956 shows off Maytree and Evergreen Cottages to advantage. The photographer is facing west looking down Church Lane towards the Greystoke Hotel. Maytree Cottage is reputed to be the oldest cottage in the village with origins in the 16th century.

Plate 236. An 8th century Saxon Church once stood on the site of St Andrew's Ferring but the present church is no youngster with origins dating back to about 1100. Major alterations took place in 1250 including the demolition of the Norman chancel and the removal of the north wall of the nave. A higher more graceful chancel was provided and the nave was improved by an arcade of four arches. The small bell-tower was added about 1800. The church was extensively restored in the 19th century, restoration being sponsored by William Henty and his family.

Plate 237. Maytree Cottage has knapped flint walls under a thatched roof. It may once have been a priest's house. In the 1930s it was also a shoe repair business. This part of Ferring abounds with mature trees and several dozen have preservation orders placed upon them. In the background is the rebuilt Old Cottage. Since 1967 Church Lane has been a one-way street.

Plate 238. Ferring Street and Church Lane just after the turn of the century with plenty of leaves and dung in the road. Old Cottage is in its original guise. To the right of the photographer is St Andrew's Church graveyard. In times past this corner was often flooded and wedding and funeral processions were routed to the church via the gardens behind the vicarage.

Ferring, Sussex.

Chatsworth Series.

This place is about a mile from where we are staying.
2nd Aug 06.

FERRING.

Plate 239. Few pictures survive which show even part of the pair of cottages which until the early years of the present century occupied a corner of the churchyard. Water was supplied to them by a standpipe in a recess in the churchyard wall. The west face of the building can be seen on the left. One brief history of Ferring suggests the lychgate dated back to 1912 but this card was posted on 25 June 1904, considerably pre-dating that estimate.

Plate 240. A 1993 photograph shows the door in The Ramblers converted to a window and the old cottages on the left demolished. There is still a depression in the graveyard ground to show where these cottages stood. A modern notice gives details of services at St Andrews Church. The register dates back to 1558.

Plate 241. Posted in Ferring on 19 April 1909 this card shows the historic Holly Lodge. Built in 1759 the cottage was for many years the village Post Office and indeed this postcard was franked and posted in this very building. The sign to the left of the yokel reads 'Post . . . .' ('Office' being hidden behind the foliage). The chimneys of the Greystoke can be seen behind.

Plate 242. The trees may not be so well pruned in 1993 as in 1909 but the entire building has been tastefully restored and the fine flints have been attractively exposed. There have been changes to the garden wall but there is still no pavement! The cottage chimney is another focal point for an 84 year comparison.

Plate 243. There is a copy of this postcard in Ferring Library with the caption 'Church Lane looking west with Old Barn ' 1910'. However the view is decidedly earlier; probably around 1905. This example was posted on 1 March 1906 and it shows ladies with aprons on, a man with a bicycle, another with a bucket in each hand and a horse and cart. The barn was saved from demolition and has been in commercial use for many years.

Plate 244. On the right of this broadly similar 1993 view is Church Cottage which is at least 200 years old and is in far better shape now than in 1909. On the left is The Ramblers with cobbles under a thatched roof. The building was used as an apple store for over 70 years. It now has 'listed' status.

Plate 245. The Old Barn, its outbuildings and an extension, is now the base of Mike Smith Carpets Ltd. The barn was linked with the Greystoke Manor Hotel and indeed under the Henty ownership it was known as St Maurs and used as a commercial riding establishment. Behind the barn is the 17th century Old Flint House; the one time home of the Kitchen Gardner of Ferring Grange, and Pembroke and Bay Tree Cottages. The Mulberry tree in the grounds of Old Flint House has a preservation order on it.

Plate 246. This photograph was taken on a plate camera in the 1930s. The rather superior caption reads 'St Maurs Private Hotel and Riding Establishment, Ferring by Sea, Sussex'. The telephone number of Goring 239 also dates the picture. St Maurs, alias the Greystoke, can be seen behind. Note the Cocker Spaniel looking-on.

The Greystoke

FG.33   GREYSTOKE MANOR HOTEL, FERRING   COPYRIGHT FRITH LTD

Plate 247. The Greystoke Manor Hotel, free house, non-residents welcome and both AA and RAC approved. This picture dates back to 1965 when some £14,000 was spent on alterations to convert the building from its former role as purely a residential hotel. Built in 1739 as a yeoman's house it was known as The Square House. As already mentioned it became St Maurs and then The Greystoke. It was once the home of Miss Somerset whose family owned Castle Goring. She was the sister of Mrs Henty of Ferring Grange. In the Spring of 1993 a new phase in its history started when it was converted to a rest home for the elderly.

Plate 248. After Greystoke Road was opened up the Greystoke stood on its own on the north west corner of the junction with Church Lane. The conservatory was converted to a permanent building extension some time after 1965 and the chimneys have been modified. The substantial east end extension is immediately obvious; a good example of the perpetually changing times. Further along the road are the Ferring Baptist Church of 1973 vintage and the Ferring Rifers Youth Centre.

Plate 249. This remarkable card was written by the son of the Goring blacksmith and sent to his girlfriend Miss Greenyer in October 1905. **He** had just marched around Ferring with the Goring Drum and Fife Band. The focal point behind the farmer and his spaniel is Church House with The Ramblers on the right; looking east down Church Lane.

Plate 250. This exceedingly old view shows a nanny out walking with a young member of the aristocracy. On the left is Holly Lodge. Church House has a door which opens directly onto the lane; now converted to a window. A delightful view in the heart of the village.

Plate 251. The 1993 photographs for this book had to be taken in Winter and although the result is generally less attractive than Spring many of the buildings cannot be seen once the trees are in leaf. All of the old buildings are still recognisable, the one way sign improves traffic flow and the main change is the new curbstone and pavement lower right.

FERRING GRANGE HOTEL

Plate 252. There is slight confusion in some minds about manor houses in Ferring. East Ferring House was undoubtedly the most important building in East Ferring with a history going back to 1565. However Ferring Grange was certainly a larger building, in the close proximity of the Church and was irrefutably the Palace of the Bishop of Chichester. It is not known precisely when the first Manor House or Grange was built. The 13th to 15th century period is equally misty. It is known that the Manor was seized by Parliament in 1647 and sold by the Parliamentary Commissioners. After passing through the hands of several noble families William Henty was in residence by 1790. In 1924 the Grange became a hotel and judging by this magnificent interior view, posted in 1928, the surroundings were sumptuous.

Ferring Grange Hotel from the air

Plate 253. This superb aerial view of Ferring Grange shows the extent of the building. The barn by the Greystoke in the background was demolished for the construction of Greystoke Road and in the top centre both Holly Lodge and Church House can clearly be identified. St Andrew's Church is nestling just behind the Grange. The area in the foreground is now covered with houses.

A Corner of the Lounge, Ferring Grange Hotel, Ferring-by-Sea, Nr. Worthing.

Plate 254. In a corner of the impressive Ferring Grange Hotel Lounge, the stairs to the first floor can be seen rising through an oak-rimmed archway. The hotel was quite popular although the 1939–45 war had a detrimental impact. However centuries of history were destroyed when on a wretched 30 October 1946 a terrible fire swept through the Grange all but destroying it. It was one of Ferring's greatest disasters.

Ferring Grange

Plate 255. This impressive aspect from the south west shows the Grange to advantage. The pointed towers and the decorative chimneys are a particularly strong feature. The beautiful surroundings, extensive grounds and well kept gardens must have been a joy to behold. The Grange created its own industry within the village with scores of tradesmen, craftsmen and domestics required to keep it running.

Plate 256. Long after the fire parts of the building which were damaged but not destroyed were converted into flats. Most of the land was sold-off for housing. This 1993 photograph shows the remains. The best focal point for comparison between the pictures is the doorway just right of centre. In retrospect perhaps we are fortunate to have even a fragment of this once grand building still standing.

BROOK LANE CARAVAN SITE, FERRING-BY-SEA.   10997

Plate 257. Far removed from life in the Grange is life in a caravan but the latter can nevertheless be fun, especially when merely visiting on sunny summer weekends. With Highdown Hill as a backdrop this was Brook Lane Caravan Site some 40 years ago. The dustbin is a nice touch!

Plate 258. The author had little trouble finding the exact spot to produce this comparison. In fact although the 'vans are larger nowadays and the styling is more angular there is not that much difference to show for the years. The ring at the top of Highdown shows signs of the 1987 hurricane damage in this 1993 shot.

Ferringham Lane

FERRING.

Plate 259. There were once a number of ponds in the Goring and Ferring areas. With improved drainage, building and the removal of the marshy saltings these have diminished over the years. There is one pond on the Goring/Ferring boundary in the Goring Gap, south of Goring Hall Drive, one on the eastern side of Highdown Hill, one at Little Paddocks and another at Kingston Manor, just north of Kingston Gorse. All others have disappeared. This location is one of the few in this volume which cannot be specifically identified; but it is certainly worth including.

Plate 260. The ultimate in rural village activity as the focus is undoubtedly bovine in Ferringham Lane. The farmer is driving the cattle past the Home Farm House/Lodge/ Cottage complex with the cottage on the left. Until the early 1930s there were two buildings (just visible) in the middle of the lane between Grange Close and Grange Park. This postcard was sent to Combe Martin in Devon in 1935 but the photograph is a year or two earlier.

Ferringham Lane, Ferring-on-Sea

"Little Paddocks"
FERRING BY SEA

Plate 261. Little Paddocks is now a delightful back-water located to the east of Ferringham Lane. The land was once part of the Ferring Grange Estate. In the centre of a ring of houses is open space and a charming pond – with ducks on it! This plate shows one of the 'composite' postcards which were so popular some years ago but the reader had to squint to see any of the pictures properly.

Plate 262. This card was posted during the short reign of King Edward VIII in 1937. On the left is Brook Lane Garage purveying Cleveland petrol to the small population of motorists. The grass verge island was where the 'centre of lane' buildings referred to in Plate 260 were located. On the right are AA and RAC signs, not for the garage but for the Ferring Grange Hotel recommendation.

Plate 263. The old Brook Lane Garage building was recently occupied by a computer and data communications company but when photographed in February 1993 there seemed to be an agents board outside. A cyclist heads south while both the Greystoke (centre left) and part of the Grange (centre right) can be seen.

Ferringham Lane, Ferring   PN2165

Plate 264. Other postcards of Ferringham Lane look very similar indeed because they merely show a line of trees rather than focussing on a particular building. Nevertheless the scene is pleasant enough. The Morris Minor car would be worth considerably more today than it was in this 1959 view.

Plate 265. A highly underrated building in Ferring is the Tudor Close. This was for centuries the most southerly building in the village and again associations with the smuggling business are well established. The building was a 12th century tithe barn but in more recent times it was a private school. It was used by the military during the war and converted for use as a pub and restaurant in 1947. In this 1960 view the sign describes the Tudor Close as a licensed restaurant (see also Plate 294).

Ocean Drive, Ferring   PN2162

Plate 266. South Ferring barely existed until 1924. With the exceptions of Tudor Close and a building or two in Sea Lane the land was primarily agricultural and very badly drained. Although the progress was from north east to south west it was piecemeal with gaps where lots were unsold. In 1961 the Midland Bank had a diminutive branch in Ocean Drive; one of the roads set out in the 1920s.

Plate 267. The shopping development in South Ferring started with the Pantiles in the early 1920s. This was in anticipation of the increase in population between Sea Lane, Ferring and the River Rife. With Ocean Drive just a dirt road, two ladies leave the shops and pass a vintage car. The date is 1929. The house on the right is still standing.

Plate 268. By the late 1930s a further parade of shops could be justified and Ocean Parade was built. This art deco era produced architecture which was far from beautiful but which had a style, indeed a fascination of its own. The 'modern' clock is a particular feature, although other eyes might focus on the MG sports car.

Plate 269. This post-war view shows both shopping parades. In design terms the comparison is uncomfortable. On the right is Beresford's Stores with a pair of traditional telephone boxes outside. At the time all that was needed to make a phone call was four old pennies and the ability to push either 'button A or B'. Sadly the fine tree has been lost but others have since been planted.

OCEAN DRIVE, FERRING–BY–SEA.   R.A.P. Co. Ltd.
London, E.C.4.

Plate 270 (Opposite top) In this 1993 scene the art deco clock has disappeared resulting in a truly timeless scene! Ocean Parade is still busy but with estate agents and banks the service industries have taken a large foothold. Behind the photographer is the Capricorn Restaurant, by the entrance to Little Paddocks.

Plate 271 (Opposite bottom) Across the road, this time looking north, the Pantiles can be seen in 1993 guise. A small garden has been created in the 'island' and the Ratepayers (Residents) Association and Parish Council tell locals and visitors exactly what is happening in Ferring via the medium of the notice boards; a pleasant touch.

FERRING-ON-SEA. PANTILES AND OCEAN PARADE.   V5483

Ocean Drive

OCEAN DRIVE FERRING-BY-SEA. 10.

Plate 272. It has been reported that when one resident arrived in Ferring in 1930 he had over 100 plots to choose from between the Church and the sea. In this stunning view from the second floor of the Pantiles, looking south down Ocean Drive in about 1928, it is clear that some plots have been built on while others are vacant. The land for the Ocean Parade shops is 'For Sale' and the sign on the right points to the Blue Bird Cafe. Even in those days there was a request to drive slowly.

Plate 273. The thatched house on the left is common to both views. Although many houses in South Ferring date back to the 1920s and 1930s some have been demolished and new buildings have sprung-up on the plots. Not all of the properties from this era were well built and some were simple timber and thatch affairs. Beehive Lane can be seen a few yards beyond the now extended 1920s dwelling.

Beehive Lane, Ferring by Sea.

Plate 274. This card was sent from Ferring to Sanderstead, Surrey in 1957 but yet again the photograph considerably pre-dates the posting date. The message is very uncomplimentary to Beehive Lane viz. 'This view of Beehive Lane is at the ugly end of it'. As originally built perhaps the frontage of the bungalows on the right was not over-attractive.

Plate 275. By 1993 any ugliness has disappeared in Beehive lane as the original buildings had either been encased in extensions, had pitched roofs added or been demolished and replaced by later designs. The lack of street lighting and pavements is so typical of the Ferring area.

Plate 276. This fascinating building is located on the east side of Ocean Drive. It is almost a 'Dutch Barn' shape. When the postcard featured in the view below was acquired its significance was not appreciated, mainly because the dwelling does not look to be old. Indeed there was nothing on the card to indicate the house was in Ocean Drive. The name 'Mina-Ha-Ha' was a curiosity (the card should say 'Mini-HaHa). This is how the property looked in 1993.

Plate 277. This postcard was posted as long ago as August 1929. What it shows is the chalet which was owned by Miss Crawford who ran a school there. Bud Flanagan and Chesney Allen, a song and dance comedy duo who became famous for their rendering of 'Underneath the Arches' and incidentally the signature tune of 'Dad's Army' lived nearby. Their pranks in Ferring included swapping house nameplates to cause maximum confusion.

Plate 278. This is the view from the southern, Florida Road, end of Ocean Drive. Two facing houses have thatched and tiled roofs respectively. It was at this location at the house called 'Florida' that members of the American 'Dodge' Car Company family lived and it was through this connection that Mrs Wallace Simpson (to become the Duchess of Windsor) visited Ferring.

Plate 279. In this view from the 1930s the two houses mentioned in the above photograph are immediately recognizable. Many other notabilities from stage and screen lived in Ferring at that time, or at least visited regularly. These names included Robertson Hare, and Raymond Massey. Other stars lived in Kingston Gorse.

South Drive

SOUTH DRIVE, FERRING—BY—SEA.

R.A.P. Co. Ltd., London.

Plate 280. Another famous visitor to Ferring was the Prince of Wales who was to become King Edward VIII but who was to abdicate as a result of the Mrs Simpson connection. This shows a not particularly well kept South Drive in the mid-1930s. The first two properties are still standing.

1190, South Drive, Ferring-by-Sea

Plate 281. A typical scene from the pre-war era with a small black saloon car in the drive of the house on the right and the customary Ferring strollers. The card has become faded with the passage of time. The houses on the right back onto the seashore.

Plate 282. The same scene in 1993 sees the right hand property extended, the second one with shutters added and chimney modifications and the left hand plots built on. The age of television has also arrived with a sprinkling of aerials.

West Drive

Plate 283. This is a great postcard for the car enthusiasts and shows visitors trying to park as near to the sea as possible. On what seems to be a cloudless day even the locals seem to be heading for the deck chairs. This is the view looking north along West Drive again in the 1930s. The card is postally unused.

Plate 284. An even earlier view before West Drive became a metalled road. Dust would be the problem in summer and mud in winter. Just beyond the third building on the right is evidence of yet another bungalow being erected. Ferring's population trebled between 1921 and 1931 and trebled again between 1931 and 1951; the figures being 256, 795 and 2100 respectively.

Plate 285. In 1993 the view is similar but the house on the right has been extended, the beams have been covered-up, new and additional windows have appeared and the wide porch has been modified. The short close on the left is called The Strand. The corner is also the only vehicular access to the south end of The Rife and the Lemon Tree Cafe.

The Beach

Plate 286. There are few greater pleasures than a walk down The Rife on a fine day. The stream flows from the South Downs around the Durrington area. Centuries ago the River Rife was an open inlet and was a well established route for smugglers. In this 1930s view development looks somewhat ramshackle. In the far left background is Highdown Hill. To the west is the derelict Park Barn.

FERRING AND HIGHDOWN HILL.

R.A.P. Co. Ltd.,
London.

Plate 287. There have been scores of postcards produced of the Ferring area showing various beach scenes. To avoid tedious repetition these views are considered to be representative samples. Here a family group prepare their sailboat while in the background a lady indulges in the Victorian practice of shielding her complexion from the sun with an umbrella!

"Martin's Retreat", Ferring-on-Sea

Plate 288. The cafe on the Ferring seafront seems to have carried a variety of names over the years. It was originally the Blue Bird and this card suggests it was once called Martin's Retreat. It is now the Lemon Tree. A Littlehampton registered boat rests on the shingle.

Plate 289. This photograph shows the cafe renamed the Blue Bird Cafe. A line of beach huts spread out towards Goring. During the Second World War the Cafe was used as a NAAFI for Canadian soldiers who were stationed in the area.

FERRING BEACH LOOKING EAST   D 16164

The Tudor Close

FERRINGHAM LANE
FERRING · SUSSEX
Telephone
Worthing 243155

Plate 290. With a bit of Union Jack patriotism on the relocated flagpole customers are enjoying their refreshment outside on a sunny February day in 1993. There have been minor changes to the breakwaters and a satellite receiving dish has appeared but the scene is basically the same as it was 60 years ago. Walls ice cream is still being sold, especially in high summer.

THE LEMON TREE CAFE

ICE CREAM

Plate 291. A relatively straight-forward view looking south about half way up West Drive. The scene is typical with neat verges, bollards or stebbles and of course another Morris Minor! With the added evidence of an Austin Devon in the distance this looks to be a 1950s view on an unused postcard.

Plate 292. Sent to Ickenham, Middlesex on 6 July 1937 the writer states that 'she will be sorry to leave here at the end of the week'. The card has a one old penny King Edward VIII stamp on it. The view is of Upper West Drive from the junction with Ferringham Lane.

Plate 293. In 1993 the beamed mock tudor house on the left can be identified and the flat topped rendered house is discernible behind the maturing trees. Although one tends not to think of these houses as old there is over 55 years between the pictures.

Plate 294. The 'cross' (x) on the postcard was placed there by the writer who in April 1936 stated 'The large place marked X is Tudor Close Prep. School. It is very pretty isn't it?' The son of the Emperor of Abyssinia attended the school. Except for the growth of trees the outlook here is very similar today and I have refrained from including a comparison picture (see also Plate 265).

Plate 295. This fascinating piece of social history shows members and spectators of Ferring Tennis Club nearly six decades ago. It seems that just before and after the Second World War there was a tennis tournament held at Ferring immediately following the annual Wimbledon competition. Leading tennis stars of the day would travel to Ferring, these included Fred Perry. The grass courts were located on Ocean Drive.

Ferring Tennis Club, Ferring-by-Sea, Sussex.

Plate 296. There were a series of postcards published around 1938 showing various views of 'Ferring Health School'. This example shows a dozen children playing netball. Some have mentioned Miss Turnbull's School in Beehive Lane but this has not been confirmed. I have no doubt older readers may be able to help identify the school and the location.

Sea Lane

Plate 297. There is a nest of elderly cottages in Sea Lane, Ferring. In the early days they formed part of the East Ferring Manor lands. The buildings have featured in as many postcards as other well known Ferring cottages. In this old view two early cottages plus in the distance Bramble Cottage snuggle on the western side of Sea Lane. In the right background is a now demolished agricultural building attached to Manor Farm.

Plate 298. By 1993 the second cottage had been extended to virtually double its frontage and since this photograph was taken a brand new cottage with front flint facings has been constructed next to Bramble Cottage. In part the flint wall has given way to modern building blocks and TV aerials abound. The side windows in Bramble Cottage are modern additions.

Plate 299. Bramble Cottage is over 300 years old. It started life as two cottages for farm labourers. This is the only known photograph showing the cottage just after the turn of the century with clearly two front doors. The urchins do not look to be at all well-off and their labouring Fathers were no doubt living at basic subsistence level.

Plate 300. This postcard shows a far less common view of Sea Lane; looking south towards the sea. It was sent by 'Vera', who was staying at Cornerways, Florida Close, Ferring on Sea, to Oxford on 28 August 1935. The footpath on the left running from the Ilex trees of Goring Hall Drive to the sea, is well used today by pedestrians and equestrian traffic.

Plate 301. In the Goring section of this book the eastern entrance to Goring Hall with its massive iron gates is featured. This 1922 postcard, which has been tinted, shows the Ferring end of the drive. These railings were also removed for the war effort and sadly all of the buildings on the right belonging to East Ferring Farm have also been demolished. Fortunately East Ferring Manor opposite remains.

Plate 302. In 1992 Ferring Church of England Primary School had just under 200 children regularly attending. The 1950s building replaced the original 1873 installation. The school is located just off of Goring Way on the east side of Sea Lane. The school has now educated three generations of Ferring children.

Plate 303. East Ferring House or Manor dates back to the year 1560. The facade is however 18th century. Previous owners include the Westbrooks, the Richardsons and the Henty family. The building appears on a map dated 1700 and a 30 feet deep well in the back garden supplied water to the house at that time. In September 1976 it was on the market for a modest £50,000. This attractive 1993 view shows the house to advantage, especially with the props of a gaslamp and an 'E' type Jaguar!

Plate 304. In the immediate post Second World War years Ferring was 'opened-up' to some degree as roads improved and new roads were built, such as Goring Way seen here. This is now the main route into and out of the village and the primary road to Goring and Worthing. The addition of now mature trees along the grass verges has helped to mellow the starkness of the long concrete road.

Goring Way, Ferring-by-Sea

11016

Plate 305. Sea Lane, Ferring twists and turns its way up from the sea and at the junction with Goring Way it turns 90 degrees left to reach the War Memorial. Thus we have completed a circular tour since Plate 224. As can be seen from this 1950s card even at this late date the road was still unadopted with deep puddles. This view shows the lane looking towards Goring.

FERRING-ON-SEA, SEA LANE.

78462

Plate 306. The same view today with the road paved and single yellow lines restricting parking. Also we see the strange phenomenon of streetlights in Ferring. The road to the beach via Sea Lane, Ferring is in the distance on the right and John Cooper's Garage is behind the photographer.

FERRING DIRECTORY.

Ferring (or West Ferring) is a parish, 64 miles south-south-west from London, 1 mile west from Goring railway station, 3 miles west from Worthing, and 4 east from Littlehampton. The Church is a small plain building, consisting of nave and chancel only. The register dates from the year 1,558. The principal landowners are Edwin Henty and David Lyons, Esqrs. The area is 1,055 acres; gross estimated rental, £2,392; rateable value, £2,055; and the population about 250.—Parish Clerk, Henry Holding.—Post Office—Thomas Winton, receiver. Letters from Worthing arrive at 9 a.m.; despatched at 5.15 p.m. The nearest money order office is at Worthing.

Bennett, Mrs
Cortis, Mr Wm, farmer
Cranstone, Mr Wm, shopkeeper
Gilliam, Mr Thomas, New Inn
Henty, Edwin, Esq, J.P.
Holding, Mr Henry, carpenter

Leggett Miss, dressmaker
Moore, Mr John, shoemaker
Penethorne, Rev G. W., M.A., vicar
Sells, Mr E. P,
Winton Thomas, shopkeeper and post-office

GORING DIRECTORY.

Goring is a parish and station on the South Coast Railway, 63¾ miles from London, 3 west from Worthing, and 12¼ from Brighton. The Church of St. Mary was rebuilt, at a cost of £6,000, in 1837, at the sole expense of David Lyon, Esq. The register dates from about the middle of the sixteenth century. Here is an endowed Parochial school. The area is 2,182 acres; gross estimated rental, £5,809; rateable value, £5,004; and the population about 550.—Parish Clerk and Schoolmaster, George Buster.—Post Office—Miss Ann Moore, receiver. Letters from Worthing delivered at 9 a.m.; dispatched at 5.25 p.m. The nearest Money Order Office is at Worthing.

Barnett, Mr G.
Belchamber, John, baker
Burrell, Sir Percival, Castle Goring
Bushby, Frederick, farmer, Church House
Buster, George, schoolmaster
Buster, Mr J., Holly-cottage, Goring
Carpenter, Charles, bricklayer
Carpenter, William, bricklayer
Dark, Mrs, Pocock Hall, Goring
Evans, Reuben, farmer, Northbrook
Hide, Elizabeth, Mrs, shoemaker
Hide, William, builder
Holloway, George
Jupp, Miss O.

Keane, —, Esq, Courtland
Lee, Mrs, Burrell's-cottage, Goring
Lucas, Mr
Lyon, Major, Goring Hall
Markwick, Josias, baker, draper, and grocer
Merritt, Mrs, Burrell's-cottage,
Moore, Ann, Miss, post office
Newland, Harry, farmer
Nye, Israel, wheelwright
Rowe, George, blacksmith
Standing, Thomas
Standen, Mrs, Bull's Head
Thorpe, Rev. E. S., Vicarage

Above is the combined Ferring and Goring Directories for the year 1872. Farm workers and labourers do not get a mention! There are just 9 names shown for Ferring and 27 for Goring.

The Seasons of Life

WHEN you were just a youngster
In the springtime of your days,
And life was for the learning
Of the world and all its ways;
The seasons seemed unending,
Far horizons out of reach,
As you revelled in the lessons
That experiences teach.

Scaling the heights of ambition
In the midday summer sun,
The pride that came with knowing
Your objectives had been won.
In turn you taught the young ones
All the skills that had been learned
Throughout a working lifetime,
And so to a rest well earned.

Now your pension pays the piper
And nobody calls the tune,
As you watch the shadows lengthen
On an autumn afternoon.
Sitting in a Sussex garden
Letting memories roam free,
If asked to live it all again,
What would your answer be?

AUDREY BIRD
Ferring Lane, Ferring, nr Worthing.

This delightful poem was published in the West Sussex Gazette in 1992. It is just one example of the many and varied talents which exist in the Goring and Ferring communities. 'The Seasons of Life' in a way reflects the essence of this book; that time does not stand still, generations get older, events continue and history is made. Reproduced by the kind permission of Audrey Bird.